Working the Web

A Student's Research Guide

Second Edition

Carol Lea Clark

University of Texas, El Paso

Harcourt College Publishers

Fort Worth   Philadelphia   San Diego   New York   Orlando   Austin   San Antonio
Toronto   Montreal   London   Sydney   Tokyo

Publisher	Earl McPeek
Acquisitions Editor	Julie McBurney
Market Strategist	John Myers
Developmental Editor	Diane Drexler
Project Editor	G. Parrish Glover
Art Director	Sue Hart
Production Manager	James McDonald

ISBN: 0-15-507475-X

Library of Congress Catalog Card Number: 99-64450

Address for Domestic Orders
Harcourt College Publishers, 6277 Sea Harbor Drive, Orlando, FL 32887-6777
800-782-4479

Address for International Orders
International Customer Service
Harcourt, Inc., 6277 Sea Harbor Drive, Orlando, FL 32887-6777
407-345-3800
(fax) 407-345-4060
(e-mail) hbintl@harcourtbrace.com

Address for Editorial Correspondence
Harcourt College Publishers, 301 Commerce Street, Suite 3700, Fort Worth, TX 76102

Web Site Address
http://www.hbcollege.com

Printed in the United States of America
0 1 2 3 4 5 6 7 8   0 3 9   9 8 7 6 5 4 3

Harcourt College Publishers

CONTENTS

WORKING
THE
WEB

PREFACE

With this second edition, *Working the Web: A Student's Research Guide* continues to be a comprehensive hands-on escort through the intricacies and rapid changes of cyberspace. Since the World Wide Web can increasingly be used to access all Internet functions, that is the primary focus of this book. I have updated and expanded the chapters on Web research to provide students with a thorough understanding of how to do research on the Web. I have refocused the chapters on creating Web pages to stress the basics of HTML and the use of Web page editors. For the convenience of instructors who use a variety of Internet protocols, I have included in this edition discussions of e-mail, mailing lists, and Usenet newsgroups. Throughout *Working the Web*, I have provided step-by-step instructions, accompanied by illustrations, to enhance discussions of Web techniques and procedures. References in the book to online sources encourage students to learn how to use the Web as a tool for understanding the Web itself. The companion Web site for this book (http://english.harbrace.com/internet) with its regularly updated Internet resources is an excellent starting point for student research and Web tutorials. Among the many distinguishing features of *Working the Web* are the following:

▼ Complete explanation of how to navigate the World Wide Web with examples from both Netscape Communicator and Microsoft Internet Explorer.

▼ Tour of the Web indicating the vast range of content available.

▼ Discussion of research techniques and resources focusing on students' needs.

▼ Chapter-length list of major research sites.

▼ Chapter on MLA and APA citation styles.

▼ Discussion and demonstration of e-mail programs, mailing lists, and Usenet newsgroups.

▼ Explanation of the basics of HTML, including some more advanced techniques such as using tables to create special effects.

▼ Discussion and demonstration of a Web page editor.

▼ Discussion and demonstration of Web page design.

▼ Appendix of student reviews of Web sites.

ACKNOWLEDGEMENTS

I would like to thank the many colleagues, friends, and students who encouraged and assisted me during the writing of both editions of *Working the Web*. Colleagues around the country who graciously reviewed the manuscript for this edition were John M. Clark, Bowling Green State University; Anne A. Colwell, University of Delaware; Marcia P. Halio, University of Delaware; Kathryn Raign, University of North Texas; and Ray Dumont, University of Massachusetts—Dartmouth. A special thanks to students who contributed their reviews for the appendix and to Amber Lea Clark who helped with locating Web resources. At Harcourt, I would like to thank the many professionals who worked on the book, particularly Julie McBurney, Diane Drexler, and Parrish Glover who helped shape this edition and also Sue Hart and James McDonald who aided in the book's production.

Carol Lea Clark
University of Texas, El Paso

Working the Web

Part I

GETTING STARTED

WORKING
THE
WEB

CHAPTER 1

An Introduction to the World Wide Web

With a few clicks of a computer mouse, you can obtain the latest stock quotes, check the day's headlines on the *New York Times*, view paintings at the Louvre in Paris, and find a recipe for cranberry-orange muffins. You do this all through the World Wide Web, a bright, colorful, and user-friendly interface to the Internet. The Web is an enormous collection of computer files called *pages*. It is a constantly changing, up-to-date research resource; a new medium for doing business; and the most powerful communications tool ever developed for personal publishing.

Estimates vary for World Wide Web usage. One group claims that an average of 96,000 individuals each day are using the Web for the first time. Another says 150,000 new users per day try out the Web. The Computer Industry Almanac estimated there were more than 147 million Internet users worldwide at the end of 1988. It projects there will be more than 720 million users worldwide at the end of 2005. The Internet's power and importance to our culture is incalculable.

A semitechnical definition of the Web is that it is a hypertext interface for accessing the Internet, the worldwide network of computer networks. *Hypertext* is a format for documents. Some words, phrases, or graphics in a hypertext document are highlighted or underlined (or both), and these words, phrases, or graphics are hypertext links (*links* or *hyperlinks* for short) to other documents. The World Wide Web is organized into pages, each with its own address. A page can be of any length or degree of complexity. Web pages allow you to use a computer mouse to click on a highlighted word or graphic and link seamlessly to another document. A user has the choice of reading a document from beginning to end or "surfing" by jumping from hyperlink to hyperlink without delving deeply into the content of any particular document.

The World Wide Web's colorful, graphics-studded, and user-friendly environment appeals to an increasing number of users who may have had neither the patience nor the desire to learn the intricacies of the older and less colorful network protocols that were predominant on the Internet before the Web was developed. (*Protocols* are sets of agreed-on conventions for transferring data across a network.) But the advances of the Web over FTP (file transfer protocol), gopher, and other protocols are more than glitz. The Web offers increased flexibility and a range of media that enhances both the impact and the content of the information transmitted to the user. Indeed, the Web began as a project designed to provide a simple and convenient way to distribute scientific information across computer networks through hypertext. This hypertext interface was fashioned to allow researchers to present their work complete with text, pictures, charts, and illustrations within a system of links that enables the user to move logically from one text section to a related section in much the same way a text note in a book might refer the reader to a related section in another chapter. The hypertext design of the Web quickly matured into a resource with simple controls that anyone can learn to use and master quickly.

Hypertext really isn't new. Print dictionaries and encyclopedias use a rudimentary form of hypertext. The Macintosh HyperCard program and similar programs for Microsoft Windows use hypertext, enabling users to select highlighted items on a computer page and move to linked documents. Recently, CD-ROMs on a wide variety of topics have begun to use a similar technology. What is revolutionary about hypertext on the Web, however, is that you can link to a document located on a computer server on your campus and then move with equal ease to documents in Boston or Brazil. Through the World Wide Web, the world has become an interconnected web of hypertext documents.

Is the Web the Internet? No. The Internet (Net) existed long before the Web, and many of the resources on the Internet are still stored in nonhypertext formats for use with older protocols, such as gopher and FTP. The Internet also includes electronic mail (e-mail) and Usenet newsgroups, a collection of some 40,000 discussion groups, which really aren't part of the Web. You can, however, access these non-Web parts of the Internet through a *browser*, a program used to navigate the Web, though they will not be in hypertext.

For a moment, think of what you know about how cable television works. The physical pieces of the Internet can be compared to all the cable and control equipment the cable company provides. The information stored throughout the Internet can be compared to the shows you receive through the cable system. A World Wide Web browser is analogous to the television. It gives you a convenient, easy-to-use interface for all the rich resources on the Internet in much the same way a good television provides you with an easy-to-use interface for viewing your favorite shows. Different television models and brands all provide the same function, though older ones may be in black and white rather than color; similarly, different Web browsers (and different, updated versions of Web browsers) vary in sophistication from text-only to full graphical capabilities. All the browsers, from text-only Lynx to graphical Netscape, access the same information on the World Wide Web.

A VERY BRIEF HISTORY OF THE INTERNET

The Internet long predates the World Wide Web. It began in the early 1960s as a computer communication network the U.S. military designed to survive a nuclear attack. Because it was decentralized, if one or more portions of the network had been destroyed, the others still could have communicated with each other. The original network was called ARPAnet (Advanced Research Projects Agency). Other networks followed as scientists and researchers discovered the many benefits of communicating with each other. University local area networks and, recently, commercial online services such as America Online and CompuServe have become part of the Internet. The most popular use of the Internet by far has been electronic mail, allowing people to communicate with each other around the world. The World Wide Web, however, with its colorful, user-friendly interface, is attracting millions of new users to the system.

The Internet has no central control. For many years, the acceptable-use policy dictated by the National Science Foundation, a major funding source, restricted the Internet to educational and nonprofit usage. In recent years, however, funding of the Internet has changed and commercial use has grown rapidly.

THE WEB'S SPECIAL CHARACTERISTICS

Until relatively recently, few ventured into cyberspace unless they were die-hard computer enthusiasts, educators, or scientists. The Internet had the appeal of access to huge amounts of information; before the Web, however, the Internet was unadorned and colorless, requiring the use of cryptic command prompts and menus to locate and retrieve information. The Web is a distinct improvement over earlier Internet protocols and interfaces in several important ways:

▼ **Hypertext** Key words or points in one document link seamlessly with parts of other documents, whether the documents are stored on the same computer or on separate machines in distant places around the world.

▼ **Hypermedia** Web pages look more like slick magazines pages than the text-only offerings of earlier Internet documents. Photos, video, sound, and interactive viewer-to-site communication make many new types of communication possible.

▼ **Browsers** Programs called browsers display hypertext files and allow the user, with the click of a mouse, to connect to a document and display it. To explore the Web, a user can pick an entry point (such as a university home page) and jump from one site to another, "browsing" at will. These programs effectively turn cyberspace into what seems like an immense disk drive.

▼ **Helper programs** Browsers launch helper or auxiliary programs, which display image, sound, and video files. This keeps the size of the browser programs smaller and increases flexibility by enabling browsers quickly to support media as they become available.

▼ **Access to documents in other formats** The Web also supports connections to documents formatted for transmission via FTP, gopher, WAIS (Wide-Area Information Server), and Usenet newsgroups, making it possible to navigate all of cyberspace without leaving a WWW browser program.

▼ **Interactivity** Many Web documents have built-in interactivity through forms that solicit responses from readers, and many Web documents include connections to Web page authors' e-mail addresses.

▼ **Self-publishing** For the first time in publishing history, individuals have the capability of publishing documents thousands or even millions may read. All that is required for publishing is a fairly modest knowledge of *HTML* (Hypertext Markup Language) and access to space on a server (a computer that stores Web documents).

A Very Brief History of the World Wide Web

The Web dates back only to 1990. Based on a proposal by Tim Berner-Lee for enhancing the Internet, CERN (the European Particle Physics Laboratory in Geneva) began work on a hypertext browser. The purpose was to allow researchers to collaborate by presenting research information not only in plain text but also in hypertext with graphics, illustrations, and, eventually, sound and video. By January 1993, fifty Web servers (or computer sites offering files in Web format) existed. That same year the first version of an advanced Web browser called Mosaic was developed by Marc Andreesen at the National Center for Supercomputing Applications (NCSA) in Champaign, Illinois; because of Mosaic's user-friendly interface, interest in the Web began to spread far beyond the scientific community. By 1994, more than ten thousand servers operated, and the Web began to attract media attention, with articles appearing in the *New York Times* and other major newspapers. In early 1996 estimates indicated more than forty thousand servers were online, with the numbers of Web pages doubling every four to six months!

HYPERTEXT TRANSFER PROTOCOL

Hypertext Transfer Protocol (HTTP) is the backbone of the World Wide Web. It is a series of agreed-on conventions and interlocking programs that make up the Web. Because HTTP is a client-server protocol, you as a user have a "client" program on your computer that uses HTTP to communicate with a remote "server" computer storing information. The remote computer runs the server portion of the Hypertext Transfer Protocol. Every document on the Web has an address (something like **http://www.somewhere.edu/home.html**). When you type in a World Wide Web address or click on a hypertext link, your HTTP client program (also called a browser) attempts to connect to the remote computer you have requested. The address you give your browser also has the name of a file. When a connection to the remote computer is established, the server looks for the file and, if it is found, downloads it to your computer. If the file isn't found, you receive an error message. Once the file downloads from the server, your client program takes over and displays the file according to its format, which may be hypertext, graphics, sound, video, or something else.

 # HYPERTEXT MARKUP LANGUAGE

Hypertext Markup Language (HTML) is a system of codes embedded in text documents that tells a Web client (browser) program how to display the document as hypertext. The codes indicate links to other documents, placement of graphics, headings, alignments, and so on. You don't need to master HTML unless you want to create Web documents yourself (discussed in later chapters). If you simply want to explore the Web and use its resources, your browser program reads and interprets the codes for you.

 # APPLICATIONS OF THE WORLD WIDE WEB

The ability to navigate the intricacies of the World Wide Web is becoming an essential skill for students because of the Web's applicability to all academic fields, the workplace, and commercial markets. The Web has become a repository for endless amounts of information on almost any subject imaginable. For example, in Thomas (**http://thomas.loc.gov**), the site for the United States Congress, you can read or download the full text of pending legislation and check on the status of bills. Because the Web can be updated so quickly, it is also an excellent source for information that changes quickly, such as stock quotes or weather conditions. The chapters that follow in this book give you a tour of the Web, explain how to research topics, and discuss major research resources.

Knowledge of how to construct Web pages with HTML transforms users of the World Wide Web into contributors. The potential power of personal publishing on the Web is incredible. Individuals are bypassing the traditional media and publishing houses and conveying their ideas directly to other Web users. After you learn a few basic codes, you can create your own pages and communicate your ideas with a worldwide audience. Most universities encourage students to register their pages; visitors to a university's home page can browse through student pages. If you wish, you can also register your pages with one of the World Wide Web search engines in order to reach a wider audience (and the automated search engines may index your site without your request).

The World Wide Web is a reflection of world culture. It's a quirky and inconsistent mix of serious research, commercial promotion, entertainment, individual opinions, propaganda, and any other type of communication humans can invent. Much out there is valuable; some of it you may consider worthless, and other things may amuse you. Certainly no one person can absorb all the sites; what you can learn are techniques that help you to find what you want to find, whether it be serious research or recreation.

ACCESSING THE WORLD WIDE WEB VIA COLLEGES AND UNIVERSITIES

To access the Web, you must have an Internet connection and a browser program, so named because it allows you to browse or explore the Web. If you are a student in a college or university, you probably have free or low-cost access to the World Wide Web and the Internet. Likely, you will connect to the Web in one of the following ways:

▼ Through computer labs with full graphical browsers such as Netscape Navigator or Microsoft Internet Explorer. If the labs use a recent version of the browser, it will display the full graphics, sound, and video of the Internet.

▼ Modem access from home with a PPP (Point-to-Point Protocol) or SLIP (Serial Line Internet Protocol) connection. Many major universities offer this to their students, though some do not. If they do, you obtain a dial-up IP (Internet Protocol) account (SLIP or PPP) and software from your university. With this type of connection, you can use Netscape or another graphical browser from your home computer. If your university offers this type of access, it also should provide you with instructions on how to implement it.

▼ Computer labs or dial-up modem access with text-only World Wide Web capability. Many universities use Lynx or another text-only browser, which enables you to access the text portions of the World Wide Web but not the graphics, sound, or video. Commonly, Lynx is accessed from a menu-based shell system. Ask at the computer help desk at your university. They can explain how to access the menu either in the university labs or by dial-up remote connection.

 # OTHER OPTIONS FOR ACCESS

If your university does not offer SLIP or PPP connections for dial-up modem usage and you want to experience the full graphical interface of the Web at home, you have two additional options:

▼ Commercial online services such as America Online (AOL) and the Microsoft Network now provide connections to the World Wide Web. Most offer free introductory hours for you to try their services. Then you pay a flat fee for a certain number of hours per month plus added charges for more hours. These providers also offer additional services, such as chat rooms (electronic discussions) and research materials that are not part of the Internet. An increasing number of cable television companies now offer high-speed modem access via a cable connection. Like other commercial online services, they offer additional services to their subscribers.

▼ Internet service providers, either local or national companies, offer SLIP or PPP full Internet access, including e-mail and other Internet protocols in addition to the World Wide Web. They generally offer no additional services that are not part of the Internet. These providers also should supply you with software and instructions for installation, though configuration of software probably will require some computer knowledge. Their fees may be lower than commercial online services.

 # USING THIS BOOK

Working the Web: A Student's Research Guide, Second Edition, is designed to introduce you to the richness and variety of resources on the Web and also to equip you to create your own Web pages. You may be using this text as part of a university class, with your instructor assigning chapters that relate to topics in your course. You may be authoring Web pages as a class assignment or using the Web to research topics related to your course subject. Or you may have selected this book as your own personal introduction to the Web. *Working the Web* is written to fill all of these roles, taking you step-by-step into an acquaintance with what the World Wide Web has to offer.

Chapter 2 (Part I) explains how to browse the Web, and Chapter 3 takes you on a guided tour of some major sites. Part II explains how to research topics on the World Wide Web and directs you to major research resources. Part III introduces HyperText Markup Language and demonstrates how to create personal Web pages. One of the appendixes features student reviews of a wide range of recreational and research-oriented Web sites. Another appendix directs you to online sources for further information.

No one text can tell you everything about the World Wide Web. This book, written in an easy-to-understand fashion, explains the basics.

The World Wide Web is an incredible resource, expanding each day in scope and substance. To the uninitiated, it may seem baffling or complicated. To the initiated, which you are soon to be, it is a tool of amazing power that enriches lives.

CHAPTER 2

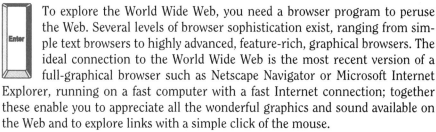

Browsing the Web

To explore the World Wide Web, you need a browser program to peruse the Web. Several levels of browser sophistication exist, ranging from simple text browsers to highly advanced, feature-rich, graphical browsers. The ideal connection to the World Wide Web is the most recent version of a full-graphical browser such as Netscape Navigator or Microsoft Internet Explorer, running on a fast computer with a fast Internet connection; together these enable you to appreciate all the wonderful graphics and sound available on the Web and to explore links with a simple click of the mouse.

Some users may not have access to a full-featured browser, either because of limitations of the computers or of the networks they are using. They are thus restricted to text-only browsers such as Lynx. Text-based browsers do not display graphics and rarely support any features more advanced than simple text display and links. Unfortunately for text-only users, many WWW sites have begun to take advantage of the innovations made possible by graphical browsers, and some Web pages make little or no sense unless viewed with a graphics-oriented browser. On the other hand, a number of research sites are primarily text, and a text-only browser will access the same textual information as a full-graphical browser.

Netscape Navigator and Microsoft Internet Explorer are the most popular of the graphical browsers, though other browsers, such as the AOL browser and Mosaic, still hold their own places on the Net. Netscape and Internet Explorer are used in this book to demonstrate navigating the Web. If you are using another graphics-oriented browser, however, your commands will be similar.

CLIENT-SERVER MODEL

The World Wide Web uses a client-server model. A Web browser is a client program that runs on your computer. When you give instructions to the client program through keystrokes or clicks on a mouse, the client requests information from a remote computer running a server program. Most obviously, you might instruct that a Web page be downloaded to your computer. A *server* is a computer that stores Web pages, and the *server program* sends the data to your client browser program.

In general, you need only know how the client part of the client-server model works, and this chapter is about that.

ANATOMY OF A WEB ADDRESS

All documents on the World Wide Web have specific addresses called URLs (Universal Resource Locators). A Web address looks something like this:

http://computer.institution.edu/filename.html

Let's go through that step by step. The **http** stands for *hypertext transfer protocol*, a designation that tells the browser program that the document you are requesting is in hypertext format. Next comes the **://**, which are simply symbols indicating that an address follows. Next are the name of the computer where the document is housed, a designation of the institution, and the suffix **.edu**, indicating an educational institution. Not all organizations housing Web pages are educational. Other suffixes for Web locations follow:

.com (commercial)

.edu (educational)

.gov (government)

.mil (military)

.net (networking)

.org (noncommercial)

Addresses also may indicate the country of origin outside the United States. These are, for example,

.jp (Japan)

.uk (United Kingdom)

.nl (The Netherlands)

.ca (Canada)

After the slash mark is the specific document or file name and the .html notation, which indicates the file is in *Hypertext Markup Language,* the language used to create hypertext documents.

Increasingly, Web addresses have domain names, or nickname addresses, which are a variation of the organization name and, thus, memorable. Examples would include **http://www.whitehouse.gov**, the address for the White House, or **http://www.microsoft.com**, the address for Microsoft Corporation. These addresses often omit the .html or htm at the end because they point to an unstated default home-page file name such as **index.htm** or **home.htm**.

 ## Accessing a Browser Program

If you are using a computer in one of your university's labs, chances are that Netscape or Internet Explorer is installed, and you can launch it by clicking on the browser's icon on your screen or by selecting it from the *Start* button. If your

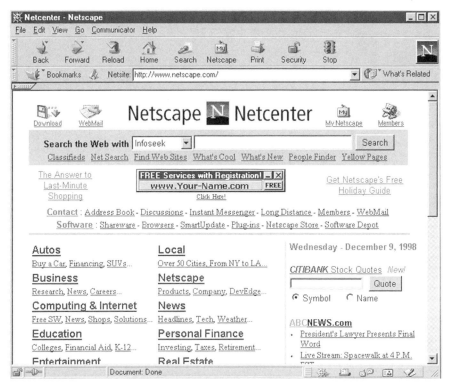

The Netscape screen has navigation buttons and pull-down menus across the top and a box at the bottom where Web pages are displayed. Copyright © 1999 Netscape Communications Corp. All Rights Reserved. This page may not be reprinted or copied without the express permission of Netscape.

Internet Explorer also offers buttons and pull-down menus for navigating Web pages which appear in the box at the bottom of the screen.

university offers a SLIP or PPP connection, you can access the browser from your home computer. You still need to install browser software on your computer, which you may be able to obtain free from your university computer center or help desk, along with instructions.

Accessing Netscape or Internet Explorer will call up the browser window, which consists of several menus above the space where Web pages appear.

 # ESSENTIALS FOR USING THE BROWSER

To begin navigating the Web using a browser, you need to understand only a few basics:

1. From any Web page, you can connect to other Web sites by clicking on hypertext links, which are highlighted (usually in blue) and underlined.

Sometimes graphics or photos are hypertext links as well. It is easy to tell what is a hypertext link (also called a *hot link*), and what is not, by moving the cursor over the word or image. If a Web address appears in the lower left corner of the screen, that word or image is a hot link to another site. If you move to a new Web page by clicking on a hypertext link, you can return to your previous page by clicking the *Back* button. You also can move forward to a previously viewed page by clicking on the *Forward* button. Thus, you can navigate throughout the Web by using these two buttons, *Back* and *Forward*.

2.   If you know a World Wide Web address and want to connect directly to it, you can do so with either Netscape or Internet Explorer in two ways:

▼ Select *Open* or *Open page* from the *File* pull-down menu, and a dialog box will open. You then can enter the address. Click on *Open* or *Okay* (depending on the browser) in the dialog box, and the browser will connect you to the page represented by that address.

▼ Use the *Netsite* or *Address* window near the top of the browser screen to connect to a Web address. Simply highlight the address in the box, touch your computer's *Delete* key to remove the address, type in the desired address, and touch *Enter*.

3.   A Web page can be of any length, though most are longer than what can be displayed in the box on the computer screen. Use the scroll bar at the right side of the screen to move up and down in a page.

4.   Watch the company logo (also called status indicator) in the upper right corner. If the logo is animated, then a transfer is in progress. Note the progress bar at the lower left corner of the page. As a page loads, numbers appear here that show the percentage of the page already downloaded. If the logo is not animated, then your connection is stalled.

5.   If you are connecting to a site and it is taking forever to connect, you may have happened on a location experiencing technical problems. Click on the *Stop* button to abort the attempted connection. Then you can try another site.

 # TRY A TEST SITE

Now you know how to connect to a Web address. Why not try one of the following addresses as an experiment?

The White House
http://www.whitehouse.gov

MTV
http://mtv.com

Discovery Channel
http://www.discovery.com

In Chapter 3 you will find URLs of other addresses you might try in your initial exploration of the Web.

 # Major Browser Options

▼   **Print**   Click on the *print* button (for Netscape), or use the *File* menu and select *Print*.

▼   **Save as**   Under the *File* menu, select *Save as*, and you can save the current Web page on a disk or on your hard drive. You have the option of saving as either a text file or an HTML file.

▼   **Search**   Check on the *Search* or *Net Search* button to receive a page of links to Web search engines. You can enter a key word in one of the search engines, and it will return a list of sites that relate to that topic.

▼   **Go**   Select the *Go* menu at the top of the screen, and you will see a list of sites you have visited in your current Web screen.

▼   **Document source**   Under the *View* menu, you can select *Document Source* and see the actual HTML file with all the codes. If you are interested in writing HTML documents yourself, you will find examining HTML-coded pages helpful toward learning how to construct your own Web pages.

 # Navigating with Netscape

Netscape has many features that make navigating the Web easier and more rewarding. Explore the pull-down menus and buttons at the top of the Netscape page. The purpose of each is outlined in the following boxes, and Netscape itself offers fairly complete documentation in help screens that can be assessed from the *Help* pull-down menu.

NETSCAPE'S TOOLBAR BUTTONS

Across the top of the Netscape screen is a series of toolbar buttons that activate features you will use frequently in Netscape.

Copyright © 1999 Netscape Communications Corp. All Rights Reserved. This page may not be reprinted or copied without the express permission of Netscape.

These are their functions:

Back

Goes back to the previous page

Forward

Goes forward to the next page

Reload

Reloads the current page

Home

Goes to your designated start page

Search

Connects to Netscape's page of search engines

Netscape

Connects to personal start page

Print

Prints document

Security

Shows security information

Stop

Stops loading of page

NETSCAPE'S PRIMARY MENUS

Across the top of the screen above the buttons are a series of pull-down menus that enable you to take advantage of many of Netscape's features.

File Edit View Go Communicator Help

Copyright © 1999 Netscape Communications Corp. All Rights Reserved. This page may not be reprinted or copied without the express permission of Netscape.

Briefly, the menus have these and other functions:

File

Accesses many features such as open page, save as (save to a file on your computer), page setup (for printing), print, and exit or quit

Edit

Allows you to copy (puts a copy of highlighted text on the clipboard), select all (highlights everything on the current page so you can copy), and find (finds a word in the current page)

View

Reloads the page, shows the page source (displays HTML codes as well as text), and provides document information (title, location, date of last modification)

Go

Reviews a list of the sites you have visited in your session, which is useful if you decide you want to reexamine a site; can go back, forward, home, or to any site on the history list

Communicator

Connects to Messenger (mail program), Composer (Web page editor), and Newsgroups

Help

Connects to Netscape's help screens

NAVIGATING WITH INTERNET EXPLORER

Internet Explorer offers the same Web-exploring options as does Netscape, but the buttons and menus are configured somewhat differently. The purposes of the primary buttons and menus are outlined in the following boxes, and Internet Explorer also offers help screens that have additional documentation.

INTERNET EXPLORER'S TOOLBAR BUTTONS

Across the top of the Internet Explorer screen is a series of toolbar buttons that activate features you will use frequently in Internet Explorer. These are their functions:

Back

Takes you back a page

Forward

Takes you forward to a previously viewed page

Stop

Stops the loading of a Web page

Refresh

Reloads the current page

Home

Takes you to the default home page for Explorer or to one you have selected

Search

Links to a search page displaying Web search engines

(continued)

(continued from previous page)

Favorites

Connects to your list of favorite Web sites

History

Displays a list of Web sites you viewed recently

Channels

Accesses Explorer's customized delivery of Web pages

Fullscreen

Displays Explorer's full screen

Mail

Accesses Explorer's mail program

INTERNET EXPLORER'S PRIMARY MENUS

Across the top of the screen above the buttons is a series of pull-down menus that enable you to take advantage of many of Internet Explorer's features.

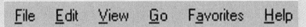

Briefly, the menus have these and other functions:

File

Offers connection to many of the main browser functions, some of which also have buttons, such as *open* (for opening the Web site), *save* (to save a Web page), *print*, and *close*

Edit

Allows you to save all or a portion of the text content of a Web page

(continued)

VERSIONS OF WEB BROWSERS

If your home computer has the capability for the latest version of a Web browser but you do not have a copy, you can download a freeware version by contacting the browser's home page. The address for Netscape, for example, is http://www.netscape.com. Commercial (not freeware) versions of browsers are also available and may offer additional features, but the freeware versions are widely in use.

 OTHER PROTOCOLS

Many documents on the Internet are not in hypertext format. Sometimes you will find that a link from a Web page will take you to a gopher or FTP document. These documents will look different from Web documents because they do not have color or graphics. Also, you can identify them because the address displayed once you connect to them will not be a Web address. FTP and gopher sites are organized by directories or menus rather than hypertext links.

(continued from previous page)

View

Enables you to control the tools visible on your browser screen (such as the standard buttons and address box) and also to open a box that displays the HTML content of the current page

Go

Allows you to return easily to a recently viewed Web page

Favorites

Provides a connection to a list of Web sites you designate as favorites; may not be usable in a computer lab

Help

Connects you to Explorer's many help screens

If you are using a library online catalog or connect to an online game such as a MUD or MOO (interactive online text games), your browser may use a Telnet client to connect you to the remote computer. Telnet site commands vary, but usually a help file will instruct you on the basic commands of each site.

You may have a specific address of a document not in HTML format. You can access these through the Web by using an address designation, specifying the type of document followed by the address. These are the main file type designations:

gopher://address   telnet://address

ftp://address   news://address

 # PLUG-INS

Plug-ins are software programs that run as auxiliaries to a Web browser and expand its capabilities. Real Audio, for example, is a plug-in that allows the computer to play sound files as they are downloaded to your computer. Some sites will display documents or files that require a plug-in to be displayed properly. These sites generally provide instructions on how and where to download the plug-in. If you are using a computer in a lab, it may or may not have the plug-in you need. Try accessing the file, and if it does not work, you probably don't have the right plug-in. You might ask your lab staff whether another computer in the lab has the plug-in.

 # OPTIONAL SETTINGS

If you are running a browser program on your home computer, you have the ability to customize a number of features.

BOOKMARKS OR FAVORITES

One of the most useful customized features of Web browsers is the Bookmark or Favorites option, which allows you to save the names and URLs of sites on the Net you would like to access easily. In Internet Explorer, you can add a bookmark to a Web page you are viewing by going to the *Favorites* pull-down menu and selecting *Add to Favorites*. In Netscape, click the Bookmarks icon and select *Add to Bookmarks*.

DEFAULT HOME PAGE

When you open a browser program, it immediately accesses a particular page. For example, by default, Netscape automatically accesses the Netscape home page. Your university labs may have specified a different page to access when launching, such as the university home page. You can do the same at home. If you would like, for example, to have your browser set to connect to the *New York Times* home page, you can do so. Under the *Edit* menu at the top of the Netscape screen, select *Preferences*. In the box under *Home Page*, type in the URL of the page you would like to access when launching your browser. In Internet Explorer, go to the *View* pull-down menu, select *Internet Options*. Under *General*, a box called *Home Page* allows you to indicate an address for a default home page.

 ## THINGS TO REMEMBER

1. Web browsers such as Netscape Navigator and Internet Explorer, programs used to explore the Web, are fairly user friendly. Once you have accessed the program, you can learn its features largely by trial and error, clicking on buttons to see what they do.

2. You can use a Web browser to jump from one page to another by clicking on the hypertext links, or you can type in a specific Web address in the *Address* or *Netsite* window and then press *Enter*.

3. Netscape and Internet Explorer offer user help. Select the *Help* pull-down menu.

CHAPTER 3

A Tour of the Web

"What can I find on the Web?"

With millions of World Wide Web pages, the Web has something for everyone. Satellite photographs, the full text of Shakespeare's plays, pending legislation, and the latest versions of programs for accessing the Web itself are all available. You'll also find bubble gum collections, baby photographs, and instructions on how to ride an elevator. The Web is a compilation of serious research and flashy entertainment. It is a place of immense variety and the furthest extremes—support groups and hate groups, illuminated manuscripts and pornography, used cars and digital cash, environmental protection papers and computer programmers' algorithmic examples. If something can be reproduced in text, photos, graphics, video, or sound, it may well be published on the Web. Or not. The Web is always under construction, with some subject areas represented much more completely than others. Everything out there in cyberspace accessible through the World Wide Web is a reflection of culture: a showcase of the best and the worst, the sublime and the trivial humans can create.

Where do you start? How do you begin to garner an impression of the depth and scope of the Web? How do you start to become familiar with the issues and controversies? The sites in this chapter represent a small sampling of what is out there. Explore these, and you will have a sense of how the Web both reflects culture and makes its own unique contribution to contemporary life.

Enthusiasts claim the Web is the most profound invention since the printing press and that it will forever change the way people worldwide access information. In the early morning, instead of heading for the curb in your house slippers for the newspaper, you can access your browser and read the *New York Times* or *U.S.A. Today*. Other major newspapers and magazines are jumping online, even though they haven't quite figured out how to make a profit from their ventures. Web-only publications such as *Salon* are developing a niche, attracted by the huge potential audience and the relatively modest cost of Web publication. And

Project Gutenberg, an online initiative volunteers run, aims to make ten thousand classic and public domain books available for downloading from the Net.

In a sense, however, everything on the Web is a publication, even if it is not organized in a traditional newspaper or magazine format. The Web is a democratic publication medium because anyone with Web access and a minimum of knowledge can create a Web presence. Pages of some Web enthusiasts, though, rival in complexity and magnitude with what major companies and institutions have compiled.

Corporations of all types promote themselves on the Web. Bank of America, Nike, Exxon, MCI, Toyota, Levi's—name a corporation or major product, and it has a Web site. Companies display products, promote their corporate image, offer customer service, and sometimes provide reader services and contests to attract repeat users to their sites.

Also advocating their positions on the Internet are special interest groups and organizations of every persuasion. During the 1996 elections, for example, major and minor candidates touted themselves online. So-called hate groups promote their white supremacist positions in technologically sophisticated sites. As long as organizations do not break any decency laws and can find an Internet provider to house their pages, they can advocate any viewpoint they wish.

Indeed, the laws governing speech on the Web still are being developed and tested. The Communications and Decency Act, part of the Telecommunications Act of 1996, attempted to prohibit distributing "indecent" or "patently offensive" content on the Internet. Later the act was ruled unconstitutional by the Supreme Court. The Child Online Protection Act (COPA) was signed into law in October 1998, making it a crime for operators of commercial Web sites to make sexually explicit material deemed "harmful to minors" available to those under 17 years of age. The Act was blocked by a federal judge who considered it unconstitutional, though at press time this injunction was subject to appeal. Still, many Web users are concerned about offensive speech and pornography on the Net, particularly its availability to children. Since the Internet's beginning, however, it has been self-regulating, and many resist governmental efforts to regulate Internet content.

The Web shows its strengths, perhaps, in sites that take advantage of the technology to offer integrated presentations of text, images, video, and sound. The NASA site, for example, displays satellite photos, a video from the first moon landing, and images from the Hubble Space Telescope. The White House site offers texts of the president's recent speeches, as well as audio from his weekly radio address.

A few years ago you may have only vaguely heard of the Internet and the World Wide Web. Now everywhere you look you see cryptic addresses like http://something.something. Now you know those are Web addresses, and you will soon be using them. What will be your personal experience when you venture out onto the Web? It is not easy to say. You may find information that will enlighten you, enable you to complete term papers, entertain you, bore you, amaze you, or even disgust you. Cyberspace has more out there than any one person can access, much less absorb. Happy surfing.

BANK OF AMERICA

http://www.BankAmerica.com

Corporations are rushing to establish a presence on the Web, advertising their products and services and featuring corporate-image text and images. How does a company grab viewers' attention and entice them to spend time at a Web site? Not much of a history exists yet for companies to model for marketing effectively on the Web. Bank of America (B of A) is one of the companies praised for its use of Web technology.

The B of A site features a "Build Your Own Bank," which allows users to customize a selection of services, articles, and other information displayed whenever the site is accessed. You can choose simply to have financial information collected that matches your personal demographics. Or you can have a checking account or apply for a loan online.

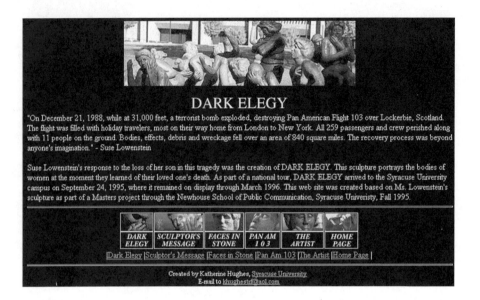

DARK ELEGY

http://www.utep.edu/~english/khughes

An example of a student personal home page, Dark Elegy was created by Katherine Hughes in recognition of the statue by that name displayed on the Syracuse University campus. Hughes's site details the history and images of the statue, which acknowledges families' grief for those who died in the crash of Pan Am Flight 103 over Lockerbie, Scotland.

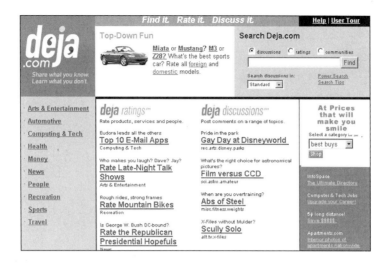

DEJA NEWS—USENET NEWSGROUPS ARCHIVE

http://dejanews.com

Usenet newsgroups is a collection of thousands of discussion groups on a wide variety of topics, both serious and frivolous, recreational and professional. Usenet is not actually part of the Web, though it can be accessed through it. If you are interested, for example, in experts' viewpoints about a recent topic in your field, consult a professional discussion group in your field. If you want to learn about bed-and-breakfast inns in Ireland or chili recipes, Usenet groups post that kind of information as well. This site, Deja News, is an indexed archive of Usenet newsgroups discussion, some 70 gigabytes of searchable data expanding to include discussions dating back to 1979.

ELECTRONIC FRONTIER FOUNDATION

http://www.eff.org

As you explore the Web, you will find many sites displaying a blue ribbon. This is part of the campaign the Electronic Frontier Foundation (EFF) and the American Civil Liberties Union cofounded to increase awareness of support for the preservation of basic civil rights in the electronic world. The blue ribbon was inspired by the yellow prisoner of war ribbons, red AIDS/HIV ribbons, and ribbons other groups display for awareness of social issues.

The EFF was founded in 1990 by Internet users concerned about protecting the Net with the principles embodied in the Constitution and Bill of Rights. Consult EFF for information about issues such as privacy of communications on the Internet, protection of intellectual property rights, free speech, and legal jurisdiction over the Internet.

MONSTER.COM

http://www.monster.com

One of the several online job banks, Monster.com offers job listings and profiles of companies who are clients. You can search the listings by key word. If you are looking for a job, you also can place your résumé online, and it can be accessed only by personnel from companies who list with the center.

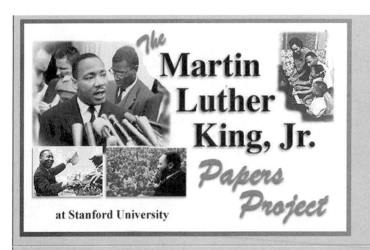

Welcome to the Martin Luther King Jr. Web Site! This site contains secondary documents written about Martin Luther King, Jr., as well as primary documents written during King's life. The folks at the Martin Luther King, Jr., Papers Project at Stanford University continuously update and improve this site. Keep checking back!

THE MARTIN LUTHER KING, JR., PAPERS PROJECT

http://www.stanford.edu/group/King

The Web site for the Martin Luther King, Jr., Papers Project offers online King's papers, some of which are otherwise not easy to find, as well as articles about King and his writings. The goal of the project Stanford University sponsors is to document King's religious roots and his relationships with other national and international leaders. By doing so, the project hopes to clarify the nature and sources of his distinctive ideas and leadership style. Eventually, the project will publish a fourteen-volume collection of King's works and commentary about them, but much of the content is available online at this site.

NASA

http://www.nasa.gov

Satellite photos, images from the Hubble Space Telescope, a video of the first human landing on the Moon, and much more can be found in the NASA pages. Through its Web site, NASA disseminates information about its aeronautics and space research. Exploring the site, you will find photo, video, and audio galleries, as well as a featured section about *Apollo 11* prepared for the twenty-fifth anniversary of humans' first landing on the Moon.

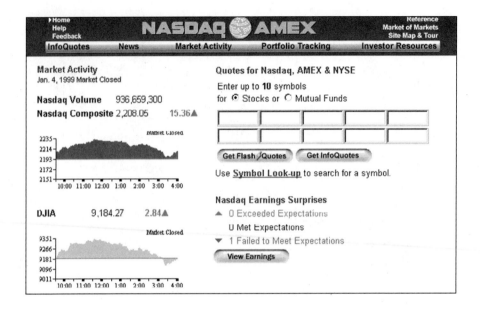

NASDAQ-AMEX

http://www.nasdaq.com

Two of the world's leading securities markets—the Nasdaq Stock Market and the American Stock Exchange—have joined together and formed one corporate umbrella, and this Web site is their online outlet. Nasdaq created the first electronic stock market. Trading for nearly 5,500 companies is executed through a computer and telecommunications network. The Web site offers current market information, including stock quotes.

DISCOVER BROKERAGE CLICK HERE.

The New York Times

ON THE WEB

NYC Weather
45° F

SUNDAY, DECEMBER 13, 1998 | Site Updated 6:20 PM

QUICK NEWS
PAGE ONE PLUS
International
National/N.Y.
Politics
Business
Technology
Science
Sports
Weather
Opinion
Arts/Living
Automobiles
Books
Diversions
Job Market
Learning
Real Estate
Travel

Clinton Says He Won't Resign Under Threat of Impeachment

President Clinton said he has "no intention of resigning" in the face of House Judiciary Committee approval of four articles of impeachment. Go to Article
• VIDEO: Excerpts From the Debate
• ISSUE IN DEPTH: The President Under Fire

Clinton's Fate Is Resting With A Few Undecided Members

The outcome of the full House impeachment vote will depend on a dozen to 30 undecided members. Go to Article

Meeting with Israeli Prime Ministe Benjamin Netanyahu on Sunday, Clinton said he would ask Congress for $1.2 billion in aid. Go to Article
• Text of Press Conference

TECHNOLOGY
With Go Network, Disney
Steps Into the Portal Wars

NEW YORK TIMES ON THE WEB

http://www.nytimes.com

The *New York Times* on the Web doesn't repeat the print edition's famous quote, "All the News That's Fit to Print," but much of the venerable newspaper is there, published in cyberspace. Like other major publications on the Web, the *Times* is free, though it may begin charging online subscription fees in the future. The Web edition is an interesting hybrid of the day's news articles from the print edition, a collection of feature stories from other sections, and some interesting Web-only innovations.

The most obvious addition is the section "Cybertimes," which has daily features about Internet controversies and innovations, along with a glossary of Internet terms and a guide to the Web. Also unique to the Web is the interactive part of the edition. Readers can post e-mail letters to the edition and contribute their opinions to forums hosted by experts in fields such as international affairs and U.S. politics.

PROJECT GUTENBERG

http://www.promo.net/pg

The intent of Project Gutenberg, like the printing press it was named for, is to revolutionize the way books are distributed. Plans call for ten thousand books to be encoded into electronic form by the year 2001. Anyone with access to the Internet can download, read, search, or analyze any of the Project's books for free.

The Project began in 1971 when Michael Hart was given a computer account at the University of Illinois. Rather than use the account for computing research, Hart decided to replicate important texts in electronic form. His premise was that "anything that can be entered into a computer can be reproduced indefinitely." The first text Hart transcribed was the Declaration of Independence. Three kinds of books are included in Project Gutenberg: light literature such as *Alice in Wonderland;* classics such as Shakespeare's plays and *Paradise Lost;* and reference books such as encyclopedias and dictionaries. Project Gutenberg is an excellent illustration of the attitude prevalent on the Internet that the free exchange of information enriches everyone.

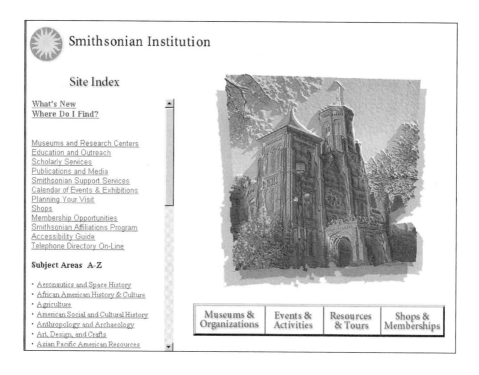

THE SMITHSONIAN INSTITUTION

http://www.si.edu

The Smithsonian is composed of sixteen museums and galleries and the National Zoo, and the Web site is designed as a companion guide. You will find information here that will help you plan your trip to any of the museums, including the National Museum of American Art; National Air and Space Museum; National Museum of African Art; National Museum of American Art; National Museum of American History; National Museum of Natural History; National Museum of the American Indian; National Portrait Gallery; and Cooper-Hewitt National Design Museum. The site also offers virtual tours, including "A Kid's Guide to the Smithsonian," "History of the Smithsonian," "Highlights of Smithsonian Institution Collections," "African and African American Resources," "Asian Pacific American Resources," "Latino Resources," and "Native American Resources." Of particular interest might be the "Computer History" virtual tour at http://www.si.edu/resource/tours/comphist/computer.htm.

SPORTSLINE USA

http://www.sportsline.com

Check the progress of your favorite team while the game is in progress. Sportsline displays play-by-play game results as they occur, as well as brief features of current sports news. Talk with fellow enthusiasts in the chat rooms, check statistics, and read about the personalities making the headlines.

Amusing the world one person at a time - visit the new Amazing GrassCAM!
☆Quirky quizzes, frazzled fish, dancing dogs, & mental musings!

Uproar presents...

The Centre for the Easily Amused!

Daily prizes in That's Life trivia game!

Grab cool graphics for linking to us!

☆NEW! You've seen the Hamster Dance,
now it's the Sparky Dance!
☆Check out our new list of dancing pages!

Fun Games & Trivia!

☆ NEW! Warm up your mouse finger for 100%!
Win prizes on Uproar Online Game Shows
Fun shockwave games in Amused Arcade
Exercise your brain with our Entertainment,
General & Sports trivia games - new questions
every Monday!

☆ Play Bingo Blitz - win cash & meet friends!

☆Send your friends free Activegrams!

☆ NEW! Torture a Fish in T-Bone's Stress
Relief Aquarium

WELCOME TO THE CENTRE FOR THE EASILY AMUSED

http://www.amused.com/

Fun and games are as much a part of the Web as serious research or business. The
Centre for the Easily Amused is a lighthearted look at sites that are on the Web
for no other reason than to amuse. Check out the link to the "Short Attention
Span Site of the Week," "Random Silliness," and "Sites That Do Stuff."

WHITE HOUSE

http://www.whitehouse.gov

The president and the First Lady extend a warm and personal welcome to cyber-space visitors at the White House Web site. Tourists can take a virtual tour of the historic house and gardens and listen to the President's most recent Saturday radio address. But the site is also a serious research site, a key access point to governmental information on the Internet, with a particular focus on Cabinet-level agencies. A subject index to publications and governmental information and a search engine provide access to White House documents. Through the site, you can send e-mail to the president, vice president, and the First Lady.

Working the Web

Part II

RESEARCHING ON THE WORLD WIDE WEB

Researching on the
World Wide Web

WORKING THE WEB

CHAPTER 4

Finding Information on the World Wide Web

The World Wide Web is an incredible resource for research. Through it you can find full text of pending legislation, searchable online editions of Shakespeare's plays, environmental impact statements, stock quotes, and much, much more.

Finding the research sources you need, however, is not always easy. Research on the Web is far more than surfing. It involves developing a purpose for your research; making a research plan; searching using the different types of access resources, such as subject indexes, keyword search engines, online libraries, and links to magazines. It also involves evaluating the material for relevance, accuracy, and bias.

The Internet is immense, and its research materials are seemingly endless. For example, if you enter the word *environment* in one of the keyword search engines, you may receive thousands of "hits," or sites that relate to that topic from all over the world. How do you sift through all of that feedback in order to find information germane to your topic? It is a problem that hasn't been completely solved on the Internet. However, some strategies will help.

DEFINE YOUR PURPOSE

As with any library research project, you need to begin by analyzing your research problem. If you are doing research for a class, your instructor may have given you the assignment in writing. Read it closely. What does your instructor ask you to do? Does he or she ask you to describe something such as environmental resources on the Internet or current treatments for AIDS patients? If so, you will be writing an *informative paper*. You will need to research the topic closely and then to summarize information related to that topic for your audience. An informative paper is more than a summary, however. You will need to focus the information in an original way that illuminates the subject for your audience.

Your assignment may ask you to argue a position or to persuade your audience to behave in a certain way. For example, you may be asked to argue for or against current practices in environmental protection. If so, you will be writing an *argumentative paper*. You will need to research your topic until you can develop a position about your topic and support that position with evidence.

MAKE A RESEARCH PLAN

Will you be using the Internet simply as one research tool along with print texts and CD-ROM databases? For many topics, some of the most current information can be found on the Web, and it can greatly enhance your information collection. Or will you be gathering all your information from the Internet? Not all topics have equal coverage on the Internet, but for many subjects (if your instructor agrees) you can collect everything you need without leaving your computer terminal. This chapter discusses the following types of resources for locating research information on the Web.

▼ **Search engines** Sites that allow you to search with one or more keywords for your subject or to explore sites by topic indexes

▼ **Librarians' subject indexes** Indexes to the Web organized by topic with Web sites that librarians select

▼ **Media links** Sites that allow you to find full-text magazine and newspaper articles on your subject

When making a research plan, you need to consider your assignment. Does it say, "Write an argumentative essay about an environmental problem such as toxic waste or acid rain"? If so, you know you need to narrow the topic from the environment in general to a more specific topic such as toxic waste and perhaps to an even more specific topic such as programs for nuclear waste disposal or the recycling of environmentally damaging substances. If you aren't sure what specific topic interests you, you will need to look first at some general sources about the environment to help you choose a topic. Several research resources on the Web can help you narrow a topic and then gather information about it.

You might, for example, examine some of the online magazines that deal with environmental topics, or you might examine the subject indexes, which might have a heading and subheadings on environmental issues. Subject indexes can be found both in search engine pages and in librarians' subject index sites. How to use these indexes will be discussed later in the chapter. Browsing these resources, you may, for example, narrow your topic to community programs for recycling.

Once you have decided on a narrow topic such as community programs for recycling, you can use the other subject indexes, keyword search engines, and media links to find additional resources. Check the list of major resource sites in Chapter 5 to see if any are relevant to your topic. As you locate resources, assemble them in a working bibliography, which will help you keep track of them also as potential resources. Remember that research is a repetitive process. As you explore sources, you may find yourself changing the narrow topic you have selected, and this will require you to find additional sources. Even when you reach the writing stage of your project, you still may need to locate information sources to fill holes in your argument. The research is not complete until the project is complete.

 # DEVELOP A WORKING BIBLIOGRAPHY

A working bibliography for a World Wide Web research project is a list of sites and their URLs, or addresses. As you browse the Web, you will see many resources that seem relevant to a possible research project. Write down the URLs. Or if you are

---

SAMPLE WORKING BIBLIOGRAPHY

RECYCLING PROGRAMS

Recycling Industry News
http://www.newspage.com

Consumer Recycling Resource Guide
http://www.obviously.com/recycle

Index of Local Recycling Pages
http://www.obviously.com/recycle/local

Recycling Laws International
http://www.raymond.com

Recycling Companies (Yahoo! list)
http://dir.yahoo.com/business and economy

National Recycle Program
http://www.em.doe.gov/recyc

Guide to Hard-to-Recycle Materials
http://www.obviously.com/recycle/guides/hard.html

RESEARCH STRATEGY FOR WORLD WIDE WEB SOURCES

1. Using a subject index (either in a search engine or a librarians' subject index), browse sites in your general topic. See what kinds of information are available on what specific topics.

2. Check online media links for articles on your general topics.

3. Narrow your search to a specific enough topic to write about in the length of research paper you intend to prepare.

4. Use one or more keyword search engines to locate relevant sites. Use advanced search options (described later in this section) to customize your search.

5. Compile the resources you have identified into a working bibliography. As you read through the materials available at different sites, continue to explore and record links they offer to related sites.

---

using a browser from your home computer, you can create bookmarks for your working bibliography (see Chapter 2 for information on bookmarks). Otherwise, if you want to return to a particular site, you may not remember the sequence of sites that led you to that location. The brief working bibliography on page 45 was compiled while researching environmental issues on the World Wide Web.

EVALUATE YOUR SOURCES

Many people in the United States tend to believe what they see in print. If information is in a book or a news magazine, it must be true. If you read critically, however, you know that all sources must be evaluated. Does a source give a balanced reporting of the evidence, or does it display bias? What resource sources are cited? What authorities? With the Internet, perhaps even more than with print texts, it is important to evaluate your sources. Undoubtedly, much reliable and valuable information is published through the Web, and you should not hesitate to use sources that, in your judgment, are credible. Remember, though, not all information on the Web is accurate. Anyone with a Web connection and a little knowledge can create a site, and automated search engines will include them in their databases. Also, many sites are commercial and may have their own marketing reasons for promoting certain information. Before relying on information, ask yourself the questions listed in "Evaluating Web Sources."

Of course, you may be intentionally studying biased sources on the Web such as home pages of political candidates, special interest groups, or companies selling products. If so, do not take their information at face value. Indeed, you can make your evaluation of biased texts part of your argument. You could, for exam-

EVALUATING WEB SOURCES

1. Who is the sponsoring organization or individual? If no author or sponsoring organization is listed, you have no way to ascertain the document's quality.

2. If an author or sponsor is listed for the site, are any credentials offered that establish credibility? Does anything indicate that the individual/organization has expert knowledge about the topic? Does anything indicate the individual might have bias toward the topic?

3. What are the criteria for including information at the site? Are the documents collected for a stated reason? If so, does that reason enhance or detract from the apparent validity of the information?

4. If it is a business or corporate site, is its purpose marketing or sales? If so, how does that affect any content information at the site?

5. What about the texts? Do they offer a balanced viewpoint? Do they cite sources for evidence they offer to support their arguments?

6. Is the site technologically sophisticated? Do the graphics or other presentation elements add to or distract from the textual content?

ple, compare what a company selling a health food supplement says about that product with what you read in your search of other texts related to that product (perhaps including scientific studies). One of the Web's revolutionary aspects is that individuals and organizations can put their side of the story directly before the public. It is part of your job as a Web consumer to evaluate critically the motivation or validity of these direct-to-the-public texts.

KEYWORD AND SUBJECT INDEX SEARCH ENGINES

The Web has a wide variety of searching tools, and more are added as the Web continues to grow. Keyword search engines are the most visible of the tools, allowing you to type in a word or words and generate a list of sites that may relate to that topic. One of the major problems with using keyword search engines for research, however, is that the number of sites and documents is so immense that the number of hits or potential resources located for a keyword can run into the thousands. Alternatively, for an uncommon topic, you might receive no hits at all. This problem led to the development of subject indexes, which divide Web resources into broad categories, such as education, health, and so on. Subject indexes are hierarchical, with major directories connecting to subdirectories. If you connect to a subject

SAMPLE SEARCH

SUBJECT INDEX

Suppose your instructor has asked you to write an essay about an environmental issue. You don't have a clear idea about a topic and decide to explore. Connect to one of the search engines that has a subject index such as Yahoo! (http://www.yahoo.com). Examine the subject entry on the *Environment and Nature* under *Society and Culture*. You can click on any of the subtopics to receive a list of sites related to that subtopic. Or you can specify a search term in the box given for keywords (be sure also to clock on the button that indicates to search only in that subcategory).

After browsing a number of the categories under environment and nature in Yahoo! (or another of the subject indexes), you may be able to narrow your topic, perhaps to recycling and then, even more specifically, to community programs for recycling.

Before you decide on a topic for your paper, however, you may want to peruse what other subject indexes have to offer because each is different. When you have a firm topic, you can try a keyword search.

Explore the subtopics in a general topic category, or use the keyword search capability only in that topic category.

category such as humanities, you will receive another menu of subtopics. A number of the indexes also offer a keyword search mechanism, so after you have narrowed a topic somewhat, you can type in a keyword and search in only part of the database.

Most of the keyword engines allow you to do more sophisticated searches than simply entering one or two key words. Unfortunately, the advanced search

SAMPLE SEARCH

KEYWORD SEARCH ENGINE

Suppose you want to write a paper about radioactive waste. Because you have a defined topic, you can go immediately to one of the keyword search engines such as AltaVista, http://www.altavista.com. Connecting to AltaVista, you receive a screen that allows you to type in keywords such as *radioactive waste*.

Typing two keywords such as *radioactive* and *waste*, however, is asking the search engine to look for sites that have either word, not both words. In this case, the search engine returns some 40,000 hits, an unmanageable number. You can narrow your search by using quote marks around the words "radioactive waste," which tells the search engine that the two words should appear together in that order. This narrows the number of hits to 28,000, still too large a number.

(continued)

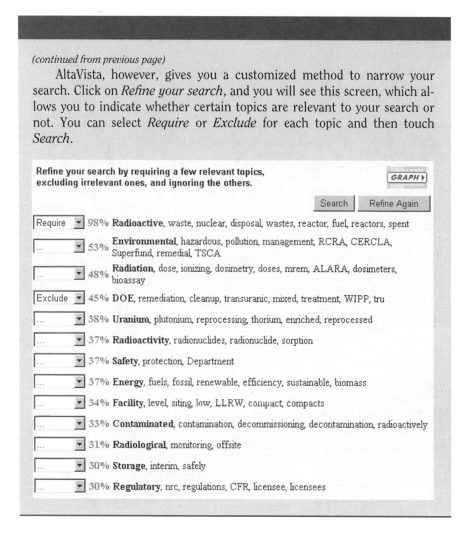

(continued from previous page)

AltaVista, however, gives you a customized method to narrow your search. Click on *Refine your search*, and you will see this screen, which allows you to indicate whether certain topics are relevant to your search or not. You can select *Require* or *Exclude* for each topic and then touch *Search*.

Refine your search by requiring a few relevant topics, excluding irrelevant ones, and ignoring the others.

[GRAPH ▶]

[Search] [Refine Again]

Require ▼	98%	**Radioactive,** waste, nuclear, disposal, wastes, reactor, fuel, reactors, spent
... ▼	53%	**Environmental,** hazardous, pollution, management, RCRA, CERCLA, Superfund, remedial, TSCA
... ▼	48%	**Radiation,** dose, ionizing, dosimetry, doses, mrem, ALARA, dosimeters, bioassay
Exclude ▼	45%	**DOE,** remediation, cleanup, transuranic, mixed, treatment, WIPP, tru
... ▼	38%	**Uranium,** plutonium, reprocessing, thorium, enriched, reprocessed
... ▼	37%	**Radioactivity,** radionuclides, radionuclide, sorption
... ▼	37%	**Safety,** protection, Department
... ▼	37%	**Energy,** fuels, fossil, renewable, efficiency, sustainable, biomass
... ▼	34%	**Facility,** level, siting, low, LLRW, compact, compacts
... ▼	33%	**Contaminated,** contamination, decommissioning, decontamination, radioactively
... ▼	31%	**Radiological,** monitoring, offsite
... ▼	30%	**Storage,** interim, safely
... ▼	30%	**Regulatory,** nrc, regulations, CFR, licensee, licensees

features vary widely from one engine to another. Generally, however, the engines offer a help screen that gives instructions on how to customize a search. These are some common search features:

▼ **Boolean operators** You use words such as *and* and *not* to limit your search. For example, if you use the keywords *radioactive waste*, some of the search engines will return hits for either *radioactive* or *waste*. If you type *radioactive and waste*, however, the search engine will look for those two terms together. If you use the keywords *Shakespeare and not plays* you will receive hits about Shakespeare but not his plays.

▼ **Quote marks** Some of the search engines allow you to put search strings in quotes, indicating that those words must appear in that order in the text. If you are looking for sites about radioactive waste, you could put the words in quotes "radioactive waste." Many search engines will recognize proper names, however, so you may not need to put quotation marks around *William Faulkner* if you are searching for information about that author.

▼ **Plus and minus signs** Place a plus (+) in front of a word, and all hits will include that word. Place a minus (−) in front, and none of the hits will include the word.

Most of the indexes—whether subject, keyword, or both—give you some kind of a description with each hit, rather than just the site name and the Web address. And most return hits in order of relevancy (as perceived by an automated program). So, even if you receive a large number of hits, a few minutes spent perusing them will generally result in finding helpful sites.

 # MAJOR SEARCH ENGINES

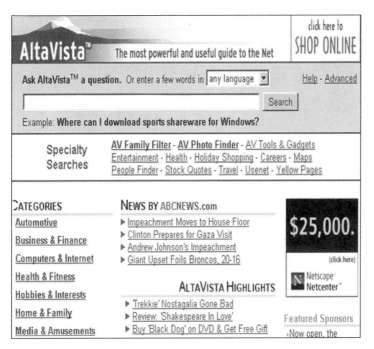

ALTAVISTA

http://www.altavista.com

A relatively new search engine, AltaVista has quickly become popular because of its size and speed. With an index of more than 22 million pages and daily listings from more than thirteen thousand newsgroups, AltaVista is possibly the largest and most complete search tool on the Web today. The search results are broad, fast, and very complete. And, amazingly enough, AltaVista is a noncommercial site, which means you don't have to wait for advertisements to load before using the search engine.

EINET GALAXY

http://www.einet.net

Galaxy offers subject indexes with links only to sites submitted to Galaxy, so listings are somewhat selective. Also, indexing is done by employees rather than being automated. Categories include business and commerce, community, engineering and technology, government, humanities, law, leisure and recreation, medicine, reference and interdisciplinary information, science, and social science. The reference section is especially useful, with links to many library special collections.

EXCITE

http://www.excite.com

Excite is another new and highly popular service that is both a subject index and a keyword search engine. This index of more than 11.5 million pages is second only to AltaVista in size of pages indexed. Excite also carries more than fifty thousand in-depth site reviews and more than 1 million daily Usenet newsgroup postings, which can be a great resource for up-to-the-minute research.

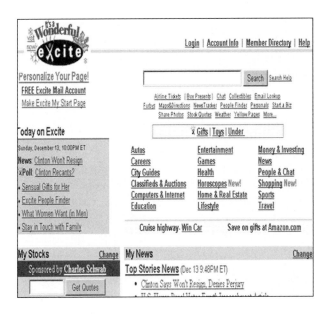

INFOSEEK

http://guide.infoseek.com

Infoseek is a search engine that allows you to search its entire database or particular subject areas, including arts and entertainment, business and finance, computers and Internet, education, government and politics, health and medicine, living, news, reference, science and technology, sports, and travel and leisure.

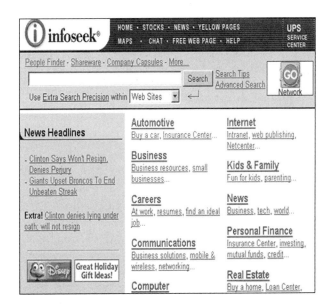

One of the most attractive features about infoseek is that after each entry, it offers a link to *Similar Pages*. If you find a listing of one useful site, you can use this feature to find others without having to determine what keywords to specify. For more search options, check the welcome screen, usually the first screen you see.

LYCOS

http://www.lycos.com

Lycos is the largest of the older search engines on the Web, and it now also has a basic subject index. The index contains entries for more than 5 million pages and generates a short blurb describing each site. The Lycos engine offers a complex form-based search page that allows you to select details such as the number of hits reported and the depth of the search.

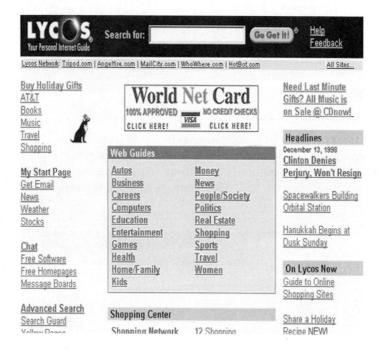

WEBCRAWLER

http://webcrawler.com

WebCrawler has earned a reputation for being fast and to the point. The default settings on the WebCrawler return a simple list of twenty-five titles pertaining to your search. This list is great if you are in a hurry and need to find some basic information about a particular topic. WebCrawler also offers a subject index and advanced keyword search features.

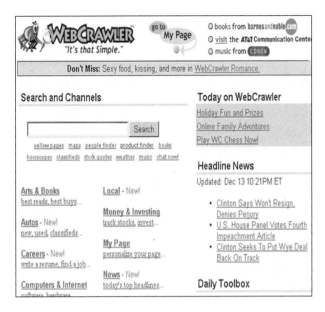

YAHOO!

http://www.yahoo.com

Yahoo!'s subject categories are arts and humanities, business and economy, computers and Internet, education, entertainment, government, health, news and media, recreation and sports, reference, regional, science, social science, and society and culture.

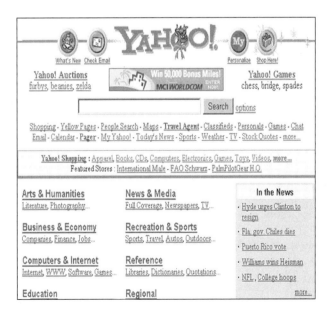

LIBRARIANS' SUBJECT INDEXES

One of the best ways to learn about Internet resources is through several major indexing projects major libraries sponsor. Librarians have personally reviewed and selected Web sites that are of value to academic researchers, including both students and faculty. These indexing Web sites are organized by subject area, though most also have keyword search engines as well. You might find it useful to bypass traditional search engines such as infoseek and Excite and to begin research for a term paper with these subject indexes. Thus, you might quickly locate the most authoritative Web sites without having to wade through masses of sites looking for the reliable ones. All of these indexes are organized somewhat differently, so you might want to browse through them and select two or three that look user friendly to you.

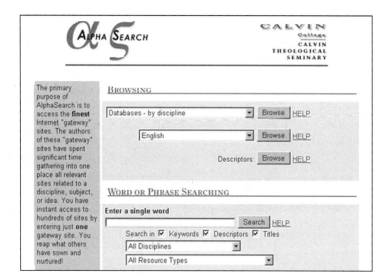

ALPHASEARCH

http://www.calvin.edu/library/as

AlphaSearch is a subject-based metasite (comprehensive site) provided by the Hekman Digital Library at Calvin College in Grand Rapids, Michigan. Users can browse "gateway" sites (which index subject areas) by resource type in any of thirty-five subjects from archaeology to Spanish or by descriptive terms. Each link has a short description and a link to a full description containing hyperlinked title words and descriptors. AlphaSearch links to more than seven hundred gateway sites organized into seven categories.

INFOMINE

http://lib-www.ucr.edu

Sponsored by the University of California at Riverside, Infomine offers links to research resources of interest to students and faculty. It is divided into major collections: biological, agricultural, and medical; government information resources; social sciences and humanities (including general reference, business, and library/information studies); physical sciences, engineering, computer science, and mathematics; Internet enabling tools; maps and geographic information systems; visual and performing arts; and instructional resources of the Internet.

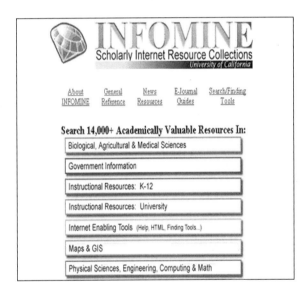

INTERNET PUBLIC LIBRARY

http://www.ipl.org

The "Reference Center" at the Internet Public Library divides Web resources into sections for arts and humanities, sciences and technology, health and medical sciences, law, government and political science, computers and Internet, business and economics, social sciences, and entertainment and leisure. The "Ask a Question" section allows the user to send a query via MOO form or e-mail. Lists and links to online books and magazines can be found in the Reading Room. The IPL is designed for K-12 students but is also useful for college students.

INTERNET SCOUT PROJECT

http://scout.cs.wisc.edu/scout/index.html

The Internet Scout Project isn't exactly a library project, but numerous librarians and educators are involved in its indexing. Sponsored by the National Science Foundation, the Internet Scout Project offers timely information to the education community about valuable Internet resources. Among its services is the "Scout Report," a weekly guide to new Internet resources read by some one hundred thousand people. It can be received either by e-mail or read in the Internet Scout Web pages. Another is the "Scout Toolkit," a collection of bookmarks to outstanding sites that index the Web.

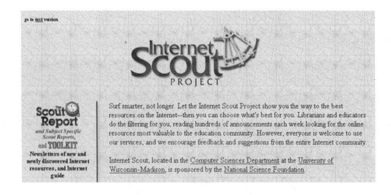

LIBRARIANS' INDEX TO THE INTERNET

http://sunsite.berkeley.edu/InternetIndex

A searchable subject index, this site lists more than 4,200 Internet resources selected and evaluated by librarians at the California State Library. The subject index is arranged in about forty broad categories with subcategories, and the keyword search index has search tips for customized searches. This site is meant to be used by both librarians and nonlibrarians as a reliable and efficient guide to described and evaluated Internet resources. Supported in part by Federal Library Services and Technology Act finding, it is administered by the California State Library.

LIBRARY OF CONGRESS

http://lcweb.loc.gov/global/explore.html

Of course, the Library of Congress (LOC) has its online catalog with bibliographic information on every book published in the United States (at http://www.loc.gov). The library also provides an extremely helpful Web page called "Explore the Internet" that indexes a wide variety of Web resources. Take a look at the topical guides to Internet resources LOC librarians prepare that include copyright resources, digital libraries, a guide to law online, and government resources. The "Learn about the Internet" section is a great place to explore if you are interested in learning more about academic resources on the Web.

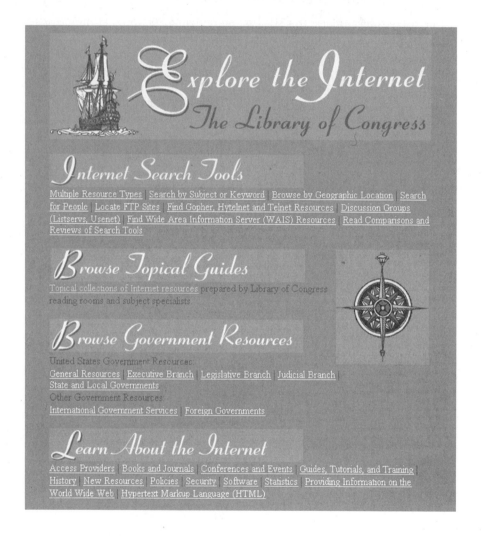

VIRTUAL LIBRARY

http://vlib.org

The Virtual Library is sponsored by CERN, the center for high-energy physics research where the Web was begun. The library is quite extensive, and not all pages are located at CERN. Rather, they are from a collaborative volunteer effort to gather information on a wide variety of topics. The Virtual Library does not offer a keyword search option, but its subject indexes are easy to follow.

The WWW Virtual Library

- Agriculture
  Agriculture, Beer & Brewing, Gardening...

- Computer Science
  Computing, Graphics, Languages, Web...

- Communications and Media
  Communications, Telecommunications, Journalism...

- Education
  Education, Cognitive Science, Libraries, Linguistics...

- Engineering
  Civil, Chemical, Electrical, Mechanical, Software...

- Humanities
  Anthropology, Art, Dance, History, Museums, Philosophy...

- Information Management
  Information Sciences, Knowledge Management...

- International Affairs
  International Security, Sustainable Development, UN.

- Law
  Law, Environmental Law...

- Business and Economics
  Economics, Finance, Transportation...

- Recreation
  Recreation, Games, Gardening, Sport...

- Regional Studies
  Asian, Latin American, West European...

- Science
  Biosciences, Medicine & Health, Physics, Chemistry.

- Society
  Political Science, Religion, Social Sciences...

MAGAZINES AND NEWSPAPERS

Fortune, the *New York Times*, *Time*, *Wired* magazine—numerous print publications are moving onto the Web, offering full-text articles in special editions or complete Web versions of the print publications. Many also offer search features for the current edition and sometimes for back issues.

Like other resources on the Web, several avenues exist to reach these publications, but no one functional and polished interface accesses all publications you might want to consult. If you know the name of the publication, try locating it directly through one of the keyword search engines. Or become familiar with the publications and links to publications discussed in this section.

SAMPLE SEARCH

MAGAZINES AND NEWSPAPERS

Browsing on the Web through a prominent magazine such as *Time* or *Fortune* may give you ideas for a term paper topic. Or you may already have a topic, and you may want to get a sense of what is going on currently in that subject area. You can connect to both *Time* and *Fortune* through the Pathfinder site, http://www.pathfinder.com.

(continued)

(continued from previous page)

If you were looking at a current issue of *Time*, for example, you might see that genetic research is a hot topic, and it may give you ideas for a term paper about the ethics of genetic research. You then could click on the full-text copy for articles on that topic.

You also can use the search engine built into the Pathfinder site. Type in your keyword in the *Search* box, and touch *Go*. You will receive a list of articles in Time Warner publications related to your topic.

 ## FINDING ONLINE VERSIONS OF PRINT PUBLICATIONS

If you are looking for a specific publication, you can enter its name in a search engine and locate the Web address. As noted in the "Sample Search," if you are looking for a Time Warner publication such as *Fortune* or *Time*, you can find it at Pathfinder, http://www.pathfinder.com. For others, try Yahoo!'s magazine list, http://www.yahoo.com/News_and_Media/Magazines, which is organized by category, or one of the other search engine's lists of magazines. For newspapers, try Ecola Newsstand, http://www.ecola.com/news; Yahoo!'s list, http://www.yahoo.com/News/Newspapers; or another search engine's list. In a few cases, publications charge for articles (usually after an introductory period), but many offer at least a portion of their full-text articles without charging.

EXAMPLES OF POPULAR MAGAZINES AND NEWSPAPERS WITH ONLINE EDITIONS

Advertising Age
http:///www.adage.com

Business Week
http://www.businessweek.com

Internet World
http://www.internetworld.com

New York Times
http://www.nytimes.com

Outside Magazine
http://outside.starwave.com

Smithsonian Magazine
http://www.smithsonianmag.si.edu

Time
http://cgi.pathfinder.com/time

USA Today
http://www.usatoday.com

U.S. News Online
http://www.usnews.com/usnews/home.htm

Wall Street Journal
http://www.wsj.com

Wired
http://www.wired.com/wired/current.html

 # THINGS TO REMEMBER

1. The Web is a fluid medium. What you find today may be gone tomorrow. If you find a useful source, document it thoroughly and keep copies of all of the relevant text portions.

2. If a URL you have doesn't work, do not immediately give up. First, check the address. Web addresses require total accuracy and are uppercase/lowercase sensitive. Often, the pages you are seeking are still on the same computer but have been given a slightly different name. Take the address and cut off the last part. See if that truncated address connects. If it does, look around at the page you find and see if your destination is listed. If this address still does not work, cut off another section and try again.

3.   If you are using a search engine, read the directions on the help screens. They will tell you how to customize your search, and this varies widely from one engine to another.

4.   Evaluate all material for bias and accuracy. It is very easy to publish on the World Wide Web, and the accuracy of materials varies widely.

5.   Be sure to give credit where credit is due. If you find a particular site useful, be sure to reference it in your works cited or reference list. Check Chapter 7 for suggested formats for citing Web sources.

CHAPTER 5

Research Resource Sites

Chapter 4 discussed tools for finding source materials on the World Wide Web, including keyword subject search engines, magazine indexes, and librarians' subject indexes. The following sites are major resource collections in their particular subject areas. If you are interested in nineteenth-century American art, for example, check out the resources listed here under "Art History," in addition to consulting the research tools listed in Chapter 4. As rapidly as the Web grows, no resource list can begin to be inclusive or up-to-date. These sites can, however, be a starting point for your research. As you examine them, look carefully for links they offer to other major research collections.

ANTHROPOLOGY

ANTHROPOLOGY WEB SITES

http://www.anth.ucsb.edu/netinfo.html

This University of California site links to anthropology sites worldwide, with sites listed by focus (such as cultural or physical anthropology) and geographic area, as well as alphabetically. It marks interesting sites as "hot."

ART HISTORY

THE PARTHeNET

http://home.mtholyoke.edu/~klconner/parthenet.html

The PartheNET contains art-related resources in the classical, ancient Near Eastern and Egyptian, medieval, Islamic and Asian, Renaissance, impressionism, and nineteenth-century American categories. Links to Web sites in each category are provided. The section on museums has links to major art museums worldwide.

WORLD WIDE ARTS RESOURCES

http://wwar.com

Market information, museums online, an artist index, exhibitions, festivals, performance arts, and academic connections are available at the World Wide Arts Resources Web site. The academic connection links the user to sources for graduate instruction, university fine arts departments, online courses, and art institutes. The search engine allows the user to browse the site for specific topics.

 # ASTRONOMY

AMERICAN ASTRONOMICAL SOCIETY

http://www.aas.org

The American Astronomical Society is the main professional organization for astronomers and offers information on education, grants, jobs, committees, and meetings. Online information can be found in the *Astrophysical Journal*, which has a search engine. Links are provided to other astronomical resources on the Internet, including databases.

ASTROWEB: ASTRONOMICAL INTERNET RESOURCES

http://www.stsci.edu/science/net-resources.html

Astro Web offers an annotated list of resources in astronomy divided into ten subject categories. The entries are tested frequently for address changes.

Biology

BIOSCI

http://www.bio.net

Primarily a clearinghouse for Usenet newsgroups and parallel e-mail lists, BIOSCI is used by biological scientists worldwide. It also provides searchable and browsable tables of contents for more than eighty scholarly journals.

CSU BioWeb

http://arnica.csustan.edu

Divided into thirty-six topical areas including environmental science, evolution, genetics, and immunology, BioWeb is maintained by California State University, Stanislaus.

 # Business

ALL BUSINESS NETWORK

http://www.all-biz.com

The All Business Network features a search engine that lists a variety of businesses and then lists links to relevant information regarding magazines, newsletters, organizations, employment, and newsgroups. The "Headline News" section has links to Ecola's Newsstand, CNN, magazines, and newspapers worldwide. The "Job Bank" contains a resource directory and articles on employment.

COMMERCENET

http://www.commerce.net

CommerceNet provides information about electronic-commerce business and technology trends and developments. To member companies it offers numerous services, but newsletter, press releases, and other documents are freely available.

THE GLOBAL NETWORK OF CHAMBERS OF COMMERCE AND INDUSTRY

http://www.ibnet.com

More than 640 Chambers of Commerce worldwide have joined the Global Network. Information from the International Business Network through the Global Business Exchange, the World Business Organization, and the World Trade Organization is available. Business-related features in finance, economics, and international marketplaces and organizations and a news and research center also have links.

HOOVER'S ONLINE

http://www.hoovers.com

Hoover's provides information about more than twelve thousand public and private companies worldwide. Hoover's Company Capsules are a free source of basic information and are useful. More in-depth profiles are offered for a fee.

INFOMINE SOCIAL SCIENCES, HUMANITIES AND GENERAL REFERENCE INDEX

http://lib-www.ucr.edu/search/ucr_sshsearch.html

This Infomine page has an extensive list of links about business topics. Check the table of contents under "B," or do a keyword search.

NIJENRODE BUSINESS WEBSERVER

http://library.nijenrode.nl

Nijenrode concentrates its information specifically for students, faculty, and researchers at business schools and has a search engine. "General Resources" includes business journals, schools, career opportunities, and news. "Specific Resources" includes finance, economics, banking, marketing, law, and ethics.

OPEN MARKET

http://www.openmarket.com

Open Market features links to many companies and corporations that have Web sites. Company information includes Open Market's history, Internet market fact sheets and business insights, and information about security on the Internet.

THE SCOUT REPORT FOR BUSINESS AND ECONOMICS

http://scout.cs.wisc.edu/scout/report/bus-econ/index.html

Written for faculty, students, staff, and librarians in business and economics, *The Scout Report* is published biweekly and offers a selective collection of Internet resources covering topics in the field. Past issues are archived.

 # CHEMISTRY

CHEMDEX.ORG

http://www.chemdex.org

Designed for professional and academic chemists, this site presented by the University of Sheffield in England provides subject indexes in nineteen areas of chemistry. Information about mailing lists and other resources are given in addition to Web sites.

THE LEARNING MATTERS OF CHEMISTRY

http://www.knowledgebydesign.com/tlmc/tlmc.html

Learning Matters is a comprehensive site that includes all areas of chemistry. Computer graphics demonstrate the scientific visualization of chemical structures and atoms as well as lab techniques. The "Software Library" features chemistry programs available for downloading. A listing of other chemistry sites on the Web is provided along with a search engine. Other features are online exercises, safety information, new technologies, and statistics.

SCIENCE HYPERMEDIA

http://www.scimedia.com/index.htm

Sponsored by ChemSW, Inc., Science Hypermedia has information regarding research, chemistry software, and education. The "Analytical Chemistry and Instrumentation" page offers software, data acquisition, electronics, data handling, diffraction, electrochemistry, imaging, standards, titration, and other areas. The "Hypermedia Index" is an alphabetical list of full-length articles on chemistry topics.

DIGITAL LIBRARIES

DIGITAL LIBRARY RESOURCES AND PROJECTS

http://lcweb.loc.gov/loc/ndlf/digital.html

This is a Library of Congress page with links to resources for digital libraries, university digital library projects, and commercial digital libraries. See also the library's "Electronic Texts and Publishing Resources" page, http://lcweb.loc.gov/global/etext/etext.html, which provides links to general resources, electronic text collections, and electronic publishers.

HUMBUL

http://users.ox.ac.uk/~humbul

HUMBUL (the HUManities BULletin board) is maintained by the staff of the Office for Humanities Computing at Bath University and resides on a server at Leicester University, both in England. Their electronic text page, accessed from the home page, provides links to electronic text archives in the United Kingdom and the United States.

LIBRARY ELECTRONIC TEXT RESOURCE SERVICE

http://www.indiana.edu/~letrs/index.html

A service of Indiana University Bloomington Libraries, this page features the Victorian Women Writers Project but also organizes links to electronic publishing sites on the Web. See the "Related Internet Resources" page, http://www.indiana.edu/~letrs/related-links/index.html.

LINKS TO ELECTRONIC BOOK AND TEXT SITES

http://www.awa.com/library/omnimedia/links.html

Sponsored by OmniMedia Digital Publishing, this site attempts to provide links to Web sites that distribute electronic books and texts, both free and commercial and in many formats (ASCII text, HTML, WinHelp, Acrobat, Envoy, SGML-encoded, etc.).

Project Gutenberg

http://promo.net/pg

Project Gutenberg offers downloadable full-text ASCII versions of books in the public domain, including many classics. The purpose is to make books and other materials available to the general public in forms a vast majority of computers, programs, and people can easily read, use, quote, and search.

Universal Library

http://www.ul.cs.cmu.edu

Located at Carnegie Mellon University in Pittsburgh, the Universal Library works toward making available "all the Authored Works of Mankind." The site includes an antique books section that features color scans of antique books, preserving the weathered character of the originals.

 # Economics

Resources for Economists on the Internet

http://rfe.org

A collection of more than seven hundred links of interest to economists has been developed and annotated by Bill Goffe, from the Department of Economics and International Business at the University of Southern Mississippi.

 # Education

AskEric

http://ericir.syr.edu

AskEric is a service the U.S. Department of Education provides for kindergarten to twelfth-grade (K–12) educators. AskEric's virtual library connects teachers to online teaching resources, and the AskEric "Clearinghouse of Information and Technology" connects teachers with network information specialists who can answer education questions for K–12 staff.

EDUCAUSE

http://www.educause.edu

Educause's focus is on educational technology, management, planning, law, and policy. The "Newsstand" has full-text articles in the online *Educause Review*, developments in information technology in *Edupage*, and news from *Educause Update*. Also provided is information on the National Learning Infrastructure Initiative, the Networking and Telecommunications Task Force, the Corporate Associates Program, Cooperative Efforts, and conferences and seminars.

GLOBAL CAMPUS

http://www.csulb.edu/gc

The Global Campus contains a variety of educational materials, such as images, sounds, text, and video to be used for nonprofit educational purposes. It offers links to similar projects at other institutions. The site is sponsored by California State University campuses at Long Beach, San Jose, Chico, and Cal Poly San Luis Obispo with the New Media Centers and other institutions.

THE GLOBAL SCHOOLHOUSE PROJECT

http://k12.cnidr.org/gsh/gshwelcome.html

This online "classroom" contains resources linking students and educators worldwide with a variety of multimedia tools. The project connects students' classroom style with resources focused on communication and using the Internet.

ONLINE EDUCATIONAL RESOURCES

http://quest.arc.nasa.gov/OER

NASA spotlights innovative sites on the World Wide Web for education. The "School and Community Networking Resources" page has educators' guides to mailing lists, Usenet, Internet, and Listservs. The "Educational Resources" page lists a wide variety of topics from the environment to Mars exploration.

ONLINE EDUCATION WWW SERVER

http://www.online.edu/index.htm

OnLine Education provides information about degree courses from accredited universities available via the Internet. Classes in marketing, health sciences, management, business, real estate, and computer-aided engineering are available. The "Business Net" has business information servers in economics, finance, and general business. The "Health Net" has links to servers in health and medicine as well as a search engine. Sites of interest include art, entertainment, news, technology, and travel.

TEACHERS HELPING TEACHERS

http://www.pacificnet.net/~mandel

Teachers Helping Teachers provides instant help for new instructors, new ideas and methods to incorporate into the classroom, and a help service for specific problems in grades K–12. Updated weekly, the "Teaching Ideas and Tips" section offers help for classroom management, language arts, math, science, social studies, the arts, special education, and a topic of the week. The Educational Resources page is a lengthy collection of links to other educational Web sites in all subjects.

THE WHOLE FROG PROJECT

http://george.lbl.gov/ITG.hm.pg.docs.Whole.Frog/Whole.Frog.html

Sponsored by Lawrence Berkeley Labs and the U.S. Department of Energy, the Whole Frog Project is an online science teaching aid for high school biology students. The virtual frog is made up of a large set of color magnetic resonance images of a frog, which allow students to explore the anatomy of a frog before ever cutting one open.

WORLD LECTURE HALL

http://www.utexas.edu/world/lecture

The World Lecture Hall contains links to pages created by faculty worldwide who are using the Web to deliver class materials.

 # ENGINEERING

CORNELL'S ENGINEERING LIBRARY

http://www.englib.cornell.edu

This Cornell University site covers all areas of engineering. The "Electronic Resources" page has links to databases and Internet-based information. The College of Engineering Web site can be searched by keyword for articles and has links to online instructional documents and class materials for courses.

ICARIS

http://www.fagg.uni-lj.si/ICARIS

The ICARIS Web site is a research network for integrated computer-aided design in civil engineering and architecture. A calendar is included for events, conferences, journal deadlines, and workshops with a search-and-add feature. The "NICE" (Networked Information-servers for Civil Engineering) contains a mailing list, server list, and resource index. The "Library" has a bibliography database of CIC papers and publications as abstracts, printable versions, and hypertext. The "SWISH Gateway" is a full-text search engine.

 # English/Grammar

Elements of Style by William Strunk, Jr.

http://www.columbia.edu/acis/bartleby/strunk

The contents of Strunk's electronic book include rules of usage, principles of composition, form, and commonly misused and misspelled words. Hot links to each section in the table of contents allow easy access to specific grammar and structure problems.

The English Server

http://english-server.hss.cmu.edu

Managed by Carnegie Mellon University, the English Server features a wide range of services, including academic resources for students and faculty, calls for papers, fiction, drama, film and television, history, technical communication, and the government. Humanities resources include philosophy, music, languages, race, rhetoric, gender and sexuality, and feminism. An added bonus is a link to download software (freeware and shareware).

A Web of Online Dictionaires

http://www.facstaff.bucknell.edu/rbeard/diction.html

This comprehensive list of online dictionaries allows the user to pick the language from a table (Algerian to Hungarian to Welsh). The index includes links to acronym dictionaires, *Roget's Thesaurus*, and synonym/antonym/homonym dictionaries. Multilingual dictionary sites are also linked, as well as an "Index of Dictionary Indexes."

PURDUE UNIVERSITY ONLINE WRITING LAB (OWL)

http://owl.english.purdue.edu

The Purdue OWL writing skills section covers all the basics, such as punctuation, sentence structure, parts of speech, research papers, citing sources (including electronic sources for both Modern Language Association and American Psychological Association styles), spelling, English as a second language, general writing concerns, résumés, and business and professional writing. Grammar exercises are provided for practice and clarity in each of the sections. The site also has links to other writing centers, resources, and OWLs on the Internet.

 # ENVIRONMENT

ATSDR SCIENCE CENTER (AGENCY FOR TOXIC SUBSTANCES AND DISEASE REGISTRY)

http://atsdr1.atsdr.cdc.gov:8080/cx.html

The Web server at ATSDR is a comprehensive environmental health information center that features hazardous waste facts and developments, environmental medicine, conferences, congressional testimony, and links to other Internet environmental resources. A search engine is provided to search the site for specific topics. Online abstracts, newsletters, fact sheets, and articles regarding the top twenty hazardous materials, exposure, medical management, and public health issues are also given.

ENVIROLINK

http://envirolink.org

Envirolink is a comprehensive information site with a library containing action alerts, education, events, government, organizations, and publications information. Environmental news stories, other sources on the Web, art, and photographs are also provided. Articles can be browsed by the search engine.

INTERNATIONAL INSTITUTE FOR SUSTAINABLE DEVELOPMENT (IISD NET)

http://iisd1.iisd.ca

IISD has a section devoted to students, faculty, and administrators of universities and colleges who wish to implement sustainable development on their campuses. Information is also given on curriculum, policy, recycling, waste management, resources, and a discussion forum. The contents include online articles from journals, key organizations, links to sustainable development sites, and governmental information. The search engine will search both documents and the glossary.

MEDICINE AND GLOBAL SURVIVAL

http://www.healthnet.org/MGS/MGS.html

Medicine and Global Survival (MGS) is an international peer-reviewed online journal that explores the consequences of war, environmental destruction, over-population, emerging infectious diseases, social responsibility, and global health. The *"MGS* Annex" lists articles available through e-mail from March 1991 to the present on topics such as nuclear energy, biological weapons, social responsibility, war, global climate changes, and sustainable development. Links to Web sites on health, international treaties, journals, newsletters, and governmental reports are also available.

 # GENERAL REFERENCE

CONSUMER WORLD

http://www.consumerworld.org

Consumer World has more than one thousand consumer resources found on the Internet. Links are provided to consumer agencies, including federal, international, state, local, private, and professional consumer organizations. Consumer resource topics include directories, information and booklets, auto and legal references, buying information, health, home, and consumer fun. Company connection links to major retailers and automobile manufacturers are also given. Other features cover travel and entertainment, money and credit, bargains and offers, and searching the Internet.

POPULATION INDEX

http://popindex.princeton.edu

The online version of the Population Index covers population studies from 1986 to the present. Included are mortality, demographics, fertility, size and growth, migration, and economics. The index is searchable by author, year, subject matter, or geographic region.

RESEARCH-IT!

http://www.iTools.com/research-it/research-it.html

Research-It! has a table with search engines for a dictionary, thesaurus, acronyms, quotations, language translators, and the King James Bible. Links to online maps, the *CIA Factbook*, and telephone directories are also provided. Additional searches include currency exchange, stocks, postal ZIP Codes, and package tracking for UPS and FedEx.

 # GEOLOGY

GEOLOGICAL SURVEYS & NATURAL RESOURCES

http://www.lib.berkeley.edu/EART/surveys.html

This comprehensive list consists of departments, associations, and societies worldwide. The "Help/Search" feature allows the user to search the library or the Internet for specific geological topics.

 # GOVERNMENT

BUREAU OF THE CENSUS

http://www.census.gov

From the U.S. Department of Commerce, this Web site covers all census information on the U.S. population, housing, economy, and geography. "DataMap" allows the user to view profiles of states and countries. The "What's New" page includes economic indicators and press releases. The help feature has e-mail and telephone numbers by specific subject, while the search engine has keyword article and staff searches.

THE DIGITAL DAILY

http://www.irs.ustreas.gov/basic/cover.html

The Digital Daily is the online tax publication from the people who know—the Internal Revenue Service. Information includes tax statistics, material, and help for individuals and businesses. Current tax regulations, electronic services, and forms and publications can be downloaded. The "IRS Newsstand" features tax tips, news releases, fact sheets, and tax supplements. The "What's Hot" page has links for help with tax questions, feedback on tax regulations, senior citizen assistance, and customer service standards.

EDGAR SECURITIES AND EXCHANGE COMMISSION DATABASE

http://www.sec.gov/edgarhp.htm

Business students will find Edgar an invaluable aid for information about public corporations. Accessible through the site are documents companies are required to file with the Securities and Exchange Commission. Many corporations also file optional documents, such as corporate annual reports.

FEDWORLD

http://www.fedworld.gov

FedWorld provides links to governmental job opportunities, the Internal Revenue Service, lists of free catalogs, world news, recent governmental reports, and access to governmental department Web sites. The search engine allows the user to search the FedWorld Web site and an index of subject categories.

GOVERNMENT RESOURCES ON THE WEB

http://www.lib.umich.edu/libhome/Documents.center/govweb.html

Presented by the University of Michigan Documents Center, this site provides comprehensive coverage of international, national, state, and statistical governmental information.

GOVERNMENT SERVERS

http://www.eff.org/govt.html

Maintained by the Electronic Frontier Foundation, this Web page links to state and federal governments in the United States and countries around the world. Where it is possible, the site links to municipal foreign governments and specific departments. Additional links are provided to meta-indices for state and local governments and state maps in the United States.

LIBRARY OF CONGRESS

http://lcweb.loc.gov

Search "LOCIS," the online Library of Congress catalog, for books by title, subject, or author. Information is also given on publications, online historical collections, and research. Also accessible is the Global Legal Information Network (GLIN) for legal abstracts and law texts from more than thirty-five countries.

STAT-USA

http://www.stat-usa.gov

STAT-USA provides daily economic, business, and trade news. Economic news releases include general economics, fiscal, financial market, price and productivity, industry, employment, and regional statistics. Databases are provided regarding international markets, exports, indices of foreign and domestic companies, demographics, politics, and socioeconomic conditions worldwide. Online copies of the U.S. budget, president's economic report, global trade outlook, and current business survey are also available.

THOMAS—UNITED STATES CONGRESS

http://thomas.loc.gov

THOMAS gives access to all current congressional legislation and documents listed by general topic, by title, and by bill number or type. Also available is the *Congressional Record* beginning with the 103rd Congress, the Constitution (searchable), and links to sites for the House of Representatives and Senate. The Government Printing Office (GPO) and the General Accounting Office (GAO) can be accessed through THOMAS.

UNITED NATIONS

http://www.unsystem.org

This is the official locator page for all United Nations organizations, such as the World Bank and the World Health Organization, and for frequently released information from these organizations.

THE WHITE HOUSE

http://www.whitehouse.gov

The virtual library of White House documents, the site also provides information about the president, vice president, and their families, and a virtual tour of the White House. A special page is offered for children.

 # HEALTH

THE GLOBAL HEALTH NETWORK

http://www.pitt.edu/HOME/GHNet/GHNet.html

A comprehensive site with links to agencies, programs, and documents covering public health, disease, and health information. The Global Health Network acts as a liaison between the public and experts from NASA, the Pan American Health Organization, and the World Health Organization. The directories include international organizations, people in health-related fields, and academic resources.

MARTINDALE'S HEALTH SCIENCE GUIDE

http://www-sci.lib.uci.edu/HSG/HSGuide.html

A "Virtual Medical Center" contains a vast amount of multimedia tools for all areas in medicine with medical dictionaries and online medical journals. Other centers, including dental, veterinary care, nursing, nutrition, public health, and allied health, have courses, tutorials, consumer information, and lectures. The "Medical Law Center" has a search engine for law and legislation, international and national law, and links to more than one hundred countries.

NATIONAL INSTITUTES OF HEALTH

http://www.nih.gov

The National Institutes of Health (NIH) is the nation's leading research center for health and medicine in the United States. The NIH site provides current news and events, as well as health information on cancer, AIDS, transplants, and consensus statements. The "Health Services/Technology Assessment Text" allows searches of databases for clinical research, prevention, and treatments.

The "Scientific Resources" page links to research, online journal, computer, and network resources.

SATELLIFE

http://www.healthnet.org

SatelLife provides electronic communication and information worldwide on public health, medicine, and the environment, especially to developing countries and disaster areas. The "Collaborative Programs" allow access to hypermail archives, Listservs, and discussions on emerging diseases, AIDS, and essential drugs. The search engine searches all of SatelLife, including the mailbox archives.

WORLD HEALTH ORGANIZATION

http://www.who.ch

Visitors can explore the status of world health, major programs, epidemiology, and statistics on the World Health Organization's Web site. "PLL (Publishing, Language and Library) Online" provides accurate health information, learning and reference material, and searchable databases. The *WHO Newsletter* provides updates on diseases, vaccines and immunizations, chemical safety, medical education, medical practice, and environmental health.

 # HISTORY

ARCHIVING EARLY AMERICA

http://earlyamerica.com

Archiving Early America's policy is to display eighteenth-century documents in representations of their original form that can be read and downloaded. The "Keigwin and Mathews Collection" features rare and historical documents such as the first U.S. Copyright Law and *The Rights of Man* by Thomas Paine. "Pages from the Past" includes a page from Ben Franklin's *Pennsylvania Gazette* in JPEG (image) format. "American's Freedom Documents" contains the Declaration of Independence, the Constitution, and the Bill of Rights. "Milestone Historic Documents" has the Northwest Ordinance, the First State of the Union Address, and George Washington's Farewell Address and Journal. Archives include a battle map from the Revolutionary War and a 1791 Bradford Edition of *Common Sense* by Thomas Paine. The site also adds a history of each document's origins.

HORUS' WEB LINKS TO HISTORY RESOURCES

http://www.ucr.edu/h-gig/horuslinks.html

Sponsored by the History Department at the University of California at Riverside, Horus offers a searchable collection of links to Web history resources. It is organized by categories, including histories of specific countries, times and places, areas of history, online services, about history, and Web tools. Coverage of history includes popular culture aspects as well as more traditional historical texts.

19TH CENTURY SCIENTIFIC AMERICAN

http://www.history.rochester.edu/Scientific_American

An electronic historical publication, the 19th Century *Scientific American* is a collection of selected historical articles beginning with its 1845 Volume I collection. The search engine for each volume returns articles by keywords for all issues in each volume.

 # HUMANITIES

HUMANITIES HUB

http://www.spaceless.com/hub

The Humanities HUB is a collection of resources for humanities and social sciences, including Internet databases, journals, and sites. Links are provided to Web sites for anthropology, architecture, cultural sciences, film, gender studies, government, history, computing, sociology, women and philosophy. Reference sites include dictionaries, libraries, and indexes.

HUMBUL

http://users.ox.ac.uk/~humbul

HUMBUL (The HUManties BULletin Board) has links to humanities resources and search facilities, including Internet bulletin boards, references, and libraries. Subject-specific resources are available in every area of the humanities. HUMBUL also has links to electronic text centers.

VOICE OF THE SHUTTLE

http://humanitas.ucsb.edu

A center for humanities research on the Web, the Voice of the Shuttle has featured works by faculty and graduate students. The "General Humanities Resources Page" has links for Listservs and Usenet newsgroups, centers and programs, and style guides; bibliographic, translation, and text analysis; and links to other humanities resources. Subject links include philosophy, history, art, classical studies, and others.

 # INTERNET, COMPUTERS, AND TECHNOLOGY

APPLE SUPPORT

http://www.info.apple.com

Apple provides access to technical information, software updates that can be downloaded, access to other Apple sites worldwide, discussion forums, and service support. The "Find" feature has an index, links to navigation aids, a visual map, resources online, groups and interests, products, and development. Apple's home page also has information about the company, conferences, Internet products and activities, and an online developer catalog.

BYTE MAGAZINE

http://www.byte.com

Feature articles from the print magazine are available for recent years along with a search engine for specific topics. A link to computer resources online is provided for advertisers such as Adobe, Apple, Microsoft, Netscape, and other major names in technology. Extensive product information is given throughout the site.

ELECTRONIC FRONTIER FOUNDATION (EFF)

http://www.eff.org

EFF's Web site contains information on freedom of speech, privacy, communications media, Internet services, and civil liberties. The "Action Alert" provides global information on legislation, censorship, and privacy issues. Topics found in the archives include activism, computers and academic freedom, free expression, legal issues, Internet information, and social responsibility. EFF also sponsors the

EFFector, a weekly online newsletter. Links are given for other online publications and information.

IBM HOME PAGE

http://www.ibm.com

The technological giant's home page features IBM news, products, and services. Articles include Internet products and services, future technology, multimedia, and software. Articles and information can be found via the search engine. Access to IBM sites in nearly thirty countries, on trade shows, and on conferences is also available.

INTERNET.COM

http://www.internet.com

Mecklemedia's Internet news and resources Web site features news, updates, and resources.

INTERNET SOCIETY

http://www.isoc.org/home.html

The Internet Society is comprised of the individuals, companies, government agencies, and foundations who created the Internet and support its continued growth. Information services include back issues of the *ISOC Forum* newsletter, articles on the history of the Internet, and international news. The society also provides access to Internet policy and standards, administration, operations, and security. Other features include society chapters, conferences, and links to World Wide Web sites.

MIT LABORATORY FOR COMPUTER SCIENCE

http://www.lcs.mit.edu

The Massachusetts Institute of Technology (MIT) has a highly technical site whose research categories include advanced network architecture, programming systems, and telemedia. Other areas are computers and people, computers and science, computer systems research, and theory. MIT also provides links to its lab services, newsgroups, and other pages.

NETWORKED COMPUTER SCIENCE TECHNICAL REFERENCE LIBRARY

http://www.ncstrl.org

This library offers a searchable collection of computer science technical reports.

SHAREWARE.COM

http://www.shareware.com

Sponsored by C-net, Shareware.com offers a searchable index of shareware programs. Shareware programs are free or low cost. The developer may ask you to pay a certain amount if you use the product after a certain period, but payment is voluntary.

VIRTUAL COMPUTER LIBRARY

http://www.utexas.edu/computer/vcl

The Virtual Computer Library is a comprehensive guide to computers and information on the Internet with a searchable database and current "What's New" section. Links are provided to academic computing centers at major universities, books, and journals with full-text articles. The section on the World Wide Web offers everything from tutorials to publishing in HTML.

WORLD WIDE WEB CONSORTIUM

http://www.w3.org

The purpose of the World Wide Web Consortium is to establish universal criteria for development of the World Wide Web. Information about Internet reference software, technical specifications, news, and updates is also available. The reference library provides a general-purpose code base for building Web client servers and sites.

 # JOB SEARCH

AMERICA'S JOB BANK

http://www.ajb.dni.us

A partnership between the U.S. Department of Labor and state-operated public employment services, America's Job Bank provides job seekers with a large pool of active job opportunities and nationwide exposure for their résumés.

CAREERPATH.COM

http://www.careerpath.com

This site allows you to search job listings by category from leading newspapers and major company Web sites. It also helps you construct an online résumé and notifies you of opportunities. Profiles of leading employers are provided.

CAREERWEB

http://www.cweb.com

Here you can post your online résumé for quick responses to job listings you search by job category, state, city, and keywords. You also can place your résumé in a database for employers to search. Some companies provide additional information about their products and services, compensation packages, and corporate background.

THE MONSTER BOARD

http://www.monster.com

Sometimes described as the "hip" job-hunting Web site, the Monster Board has more than 220,000 résumés in its database and more than 50,000 jobs. Post your résumé, and the Monster Board notifies you when a new job listing matches your qualifications.

ONLINE CAREER CENTER

http://www.occ.com

More than 4,500 member companies, including most of the *Fortune* 500, list job openings at this site. You also can post your résumé for member companies to examine.

 # LAW/LEGAL

FINDLAW

http://www.findlaw.com

Modeled on Yahoo!'s organization, FindLaw has twelve subject categories and numerous subcategories, as well as a searchable index.

GUIDE TO LAW ONLINE

http://lcweb2.loc.gov/glin/worldlaw.html

Sponsored by the U.S. Law Library of Congress for the Global Legal Information Network (GLIN), this site is an annotated hypertext guide to free online sources of information worldwide on government and law. All sites have been screened by the GLIN staff for usefulness and reliability.

INTERNET LAW LIBRARY

http://law.house.gov

The Internet Law Library (formerly the U.S. House of Representatives Internet Law Library) was begun by the U.S. House of Representatives Law Revision Counsel Office. The aim of the site is to make the law (particularly the U.S. Code) available to the public. It is organized geographically and by subject.

INTERNET LEGAL RESOURCE GUIDE

http://www.ilrg.com

The Internet Legal Resource Guide is a comprehensive collection of information concerning the law for both laypeople and legal professionals. Features include news, information on legal study abroad, legal Internet references and resources, and a government resources index. Information on law firms and law schools, a law student services index, and a searchable directory are also offered. The guide has additional links to newsgroups, legal indexes, search engines, court laws and rules, and federal judicial decisions.

 # LIBRARIES

UNCOVERWEB

http://uncweb.carl.org

UncoverWeb offers a searchable database of thousands of journals and magazines. You can order articles to be faxed (for a fee) to you, or you can copy the citation and find the articles in your own library or through interlibrary loan. The site is a service of the Colorado Association of Research Libraries.

INFOMINE

http://lib-www.ucr.edu

A comprehensive Internet resource collection provided by the University of California at Riverside, Infomine offers links to major Web sites for all main academic areas. The sites have been specially selected for their usefulness to university faculty and students.

INTERNET PUBLIC LIBRARY

http://www.ipl.org

This site calls itself the "first public library of the Internet" and provides librarians to answer reference questions. Links to Internet resources include magazines, newspapers, and books.

THE LIBRARY OF CONGRESS

http://www.loc.gov

This extensive online catalog lists books published in the United States in recent years. Also, a broad list of Web resources is organized by category.

VIRTUAL LIBRARY

http://www.w3.org/vl

The Virtual Library is a collaborative volunteer effort to provide information on a wide variety of topics. It is sponsored by CERN, the center for high-energy physics research where the World Wide Web originated.

 # MATHEMATICS

ELECTRONIC JOURNAL OF UNDERGRADUATE MATHEMATICS

http://math.furman.edu/~mwoodard/fuejum/welcome.html

This online journal publishes papers written by undergraduate students under the sponsorship of full-time faculty. Two journals are available, as well as links to peer-reviewed professional mathematical journals. As an aid to writing articles, the journal also includes a searchable quotations page.

E-MATH

http://e-math.ams.org

From the American Mathematical Society (AMS), e-MATH provides information about the AMS, bookstores listing books and journals, conferences and meetings, ethical guidelines, job opportunities, and education. Access is available to the math digest with summaries of articles, math news, and updates. Bulletin articles from 1992 through 1995 are provided and can be searched.

MATH ARCHIVES

http://archives.math.utk.edu

The Math Archives provides access to a wide variety of mathematical resources on the Internet, such as math journals, software, texts, and teaching materials. Educational resources include calculus online, lessons, tutorials, lecture notes, math for grades K–12, and college math. Links to math-related Web sites also are given.

 # MEDIA

AMERICAN JOURNALISM REVIEW NEWS LINK

http://www.newslink.org/news.html

Links to more than 3,500 online newspapers in the United States are provided.

CBS.COM

http://www.cbs.com

CBS offers information about current entertainment programming, as well as current news, sports, and weather. It gives links to local CBS-affiliate stations.

CNET: THE COMPUTER NETWORK

http://www.cnet.com

Cnet is a source for news about computers, the Internet, and digital technologies. It was offered free at press time, though registration is requested.

CNN INTERACTIVE

http://www.cnn.com

Here you can browse today's headlines, search archives by keyword for articles specially written for CNN Interactive, and see transcripts of stories aired on CNN.

ECOLA NEWSSTAND

http://www.ecola.com

Ecola indexes more than 6,300 newspapers and magazines. It has full-text archives of newspapers and links to home pages of magazines, which generally do not offer full-text articles.

Lists of Newspaper and Periodical Resources on the Internet

http://lcweb.loc.gov/rr/news/lists.html

This Library of Congress list of online media includes newspapers, news services, periodicals, and other collections of links to Web media.

Mediainfo Links: Editor and Publisher's Online Media Directory

http://www.mediainfo.com/emedia

This is an extensive guide to home pages of media outlets throughout the world, though many are not full text. It includes associations, city guides, magazines, newspapers, radio, syndicates, and television.

MSNBC

http://www.msnbc.com

A joint venture of NBC News and the Microsoft Network, MSNBC is news oriented, covering the top stories of the day and offering features on popular topics such as business, sports, and technology.

NewsLibrary

http://newslibrary.com

This searchable archive of forty-one major online United States newspapers is provided by Knight-Ridder.

Pathfinder (Time Warner)

http://www.pathfinder.com

Pathfinder offers searches of *Time, Fortune, People,* and other Time Warner publications. It also links to Web sites with current information about such topics as Net culture, travel, health, entertainment, sports, and business.

PBS Online

http://www.pbs.org

PBS is divided into neighborhoods (sites) including "News and Views," "Learn with PBS," history, science, and technology. It offers information and features related to PBS television shows and also independent Web-only content.

TechWeb

http://www.techweb.com

TechWeb provides searchable online publications focusing on computers, electronics, information technology, and the Internet.

 # Medicine

Doctor's Guide to the Internet

http://www.pslgroup.com/docguide.htm

The Doctor's Guide provides current news and developments in the world of medicine from treatments to pharmaceuticals. "New Medical Sites" provides links to Internet sources for specific diseases and conditions. A database of medical resources by type, such as Listservs, associations, journals, schools, and medications, is available. The search feature searches the entire site and provides access to the major Internet search engines.

HyperDOC (National Library of Medicine)

http://www.nlm.nih.gov

HyperDOC is the National Library of Medicine's (NLM) access to online services for clinical information, databases, publications, medical history, and biotechnology. "NLM Services" provides links to sites on HIV/AIDS, biotechnology, toxicology, environmental health, research, and medicine. NLM publications, including fact sheets, newsletters, bulletins, and published reports, are provided online and can be ordered in printed form.

Medscape

http://www.medscape.com

Medscape has an enormous amount of medical information and features peer-reviewed articles, news, self-assessment, and a search engine. The search option allows you to limit the time of the article (i.e., the oldest article available on the topic to the most recent) and returns articles from magazines, journals, and the *Morbidity and Mortality Weekly Report.*

MEDWEB

http://www.medweb.emory.edu

MedWeb is provided by Emory University Health Sciences Center Library and lists medical topics from aerospace medicine to veterinary medicine. Each topic covers clinical practice information, conferences, consumer health, documents, electronic publications, and links to other sites. MedWeb also has a keyword search engine.

PEDIATRIC DATABASE (PEDBASE) HOMEPAGE

http://www.icondata.com/health/pedbase

PEDBASE is a medical database that provides information on various pediatric diseases. Diseases and disorders are listed alphabetically. Each page lists a definition of the disease/disorder, epidemiology, pathogens, clinical features, complications, diagnosis, management, therapy, and prognosis. When available, links to Web sites on specific diseases are provided. A shareware version of the database is available.

 # MOVIES

THE MOVIE DATABASE

http://us.imdb.com

The Internet Movie Database is a comprehensive database of movies, film, and television programs. The site has a powerful search engine that can correlate information about actors and actresses, producers, directors, writers, editors, cinematographers, costume designers, movie titles, release dates, and running times. It even provides complete information about movie plots, bloopers, cast, and credits.

 # PERSONAL HOME PAGES WORLDWIDE

PERSONAL PAGES WORLDWIDE: COLLEGE AND UNIVERSITY COLLECTIONS

http://www.utexas.edu/world/personal

This site links to collections of personal pages at colleges and universities worldwide. It provides a form to add your university to the collection.

YAHOO!'S LIST OF PERSONAL HOME PAGES

http://www.yahoo.com/Society_and_Culture/People/Personal_Home
_Pages/

This list links to more than fifty thousand home pages in the United States. Yahoo! also maintains lists of home pages in other countries. You can suggest adding your home page to the list by clicking on "Suggest a Site" and following the directions.

 # PHILOSOPHY

GUIDE TO PHILOSOPHY ON THE INTERNET

http://www.earlham.edu/~peters/philinks.htm

Authored by Peter Suber, professor of philosophy at Earlham College (Richmond, Indiana), this guide indexes philosophy resources on the Web in fourteen major categories, including general guides, topics, e-texts, jobs, associations, bibliographies, mailing lists, newsgroups, and philosophers. Suber marks recommended sites with a red star.

PHILOSOPHY AROUND THE WEB

http://users.ox.ac.uk/~worc0337/phil_index.html

Created and maintained by Peter J. King, philosophy lecturer at the University of North London, this site offers topical coverage of more than fifteen subjects, links to Web pages for philosophers both living and dead, university pages, journals, discussion lists, conference announcements, and job lists.

 # PHYSICS

AMERICAN INSTITUTE OF PHYSICS

http://www.aip.org

The *APL Online* is a weekly hypertext version of the printed journal *Applied Physics Letters* and has information on research in science, engineering, and technology. Links also are provided to electronic newsletters and bulletins, as well as to other Web physics sites.

PSYCHOLOGY

CLINICAL PSYCHOLOGY RESOURCES

http://www.psychologie.uni-bonn.de/kap/links_20.htm

The contents here include articles on disorders, assessment, behavioral medicine, and psychotherapy. Links to online journals and sites for psychology-related organizations are provided. The search engine will keyword search the American Psychological Association server index for articles and books.

MENTAL HEALTH NET PROFESSIONAL RESOURCES

http://www.cmhc.com/prof.htm

This site offers annotated rated resources for mental health professionals in more than twenty-five subject categories. It also gives information about professional associations, academic departments, employment, mailing lists, and newsgroups.

PSYCH WEB

http://www.psychwww.com

At Psych Web, two classic online books, Freud's *The Interpretation of Dreams* and William James's *The Varieties of Religious Experience*, can be searched by tables of contents. The collection of brochures and articles includes counseling information from universities, reports from the National Institutes of Health, and articles from *Psychiatric Times*. Links to psychology journals and relevant Web psychology sites are available.

 # RELIGION

COMPARATIVE RELIGION

http://www.academicinfo.net/religindex.html

The Comparative Religion site is a large comprehensive references and resources list to all religions and aspects of religion. The general directories and pages cover societies and associations, world scriptures, religious tolerance, and paganism.

"Art and Religion" includes Asian, Egyptian, Roman, Greek, Islamic, Christian, and Jewish art.

 # SCIENCE

DISCOVERY CHANNEL ONLINE

http://www.discovery.com

The online version of the Discovery Channel found on television has the general science categories of history, nature, science, people, exploration, and technology. It also features a search engine that can use keywords or key phrases.

DISCOVER MAGAZINE

http://www.dc.enews.com/magazines/discover

An abbreviated version of the newsstand issue, *Discover Magazine* online includes the text from feature articles. The "Archive Library" allows the user to browse past issues and search for articles.

NATIONAL ACADEMY OF SCIENCES

http://www.nas.edu

The National Academy of Engineering, the Institute of Medicine, and the National Research Council have combined to produce a comprehensive research site for science and engineering. The site's focus is on math and science education and international programs. "On-Line Books and Executive Summaries" contains a search engine for full-text articles. The "Career Planning Center" page features job openings and information on education. The "Program Units" page has links to science institutes and organizations.

NETWORK SCIENCE

http://www.netsci.org

NetSci focuses on biotechnological articles, literature, industry and product updates, genome research, and chemistry. The monthly online magazine features articles and general industry information. Past issues are archived at the site. "Biotech Focus" provides information about new treatments, pharmaceuticals, and therapies. Links to other major science Web sites also are given.

SOCIAL SCIENCE

POLITICAL SCIENCE RESOURCES ON THE WEB

http://www.lib.umich.edu/libhome/Documents.center/polisci.html

Maintained by the University of Michigan, the Documents Center has links to Web sites in all areas of political and social sciences, including area studies, political methodology, political theory, foreign politics, and international relations. Additional links include reference source sites, statistics, dissertations, Internet guides, periodicals, think tanks, and news sources. Class assignments on various topics in political science are accessible from several universities.

PRAXIS

http://caster.ssw.upenn.edu/~restes/praxis.html

PRAXIS is a large collection of international articles on social and economic development from the individual and group level to the world-building level. Links are provided to other social science resources and international organizations. Resources areas range from agriculture to urban development and include population groups.

SOCIAL SCIENCE INFORMATION GATEWAY (SOSIG)

http://sosig.esrc.bris.ac.uk/welcome.html

SOSIG features a searchable database that returns available Web sites with a brief description based on a keyword or key phrase. World resources are listed alphabetically from accountancy through statistics with links to Internet sites. Other features include information on workshops and material available for downloading.

 # SPORTS

ESPN.COM

http://espn.go.com

News and information about many popular sports and sports personalities is brought to you live over the Web division of the giant ESPN sports network. You can select from a list of sports and events, find out what is going on behind the scenes, and catch up on all of the latest sports talk.

OUTSIDE ONLINE

http://outside.starwave.com:80

This online magazine for outdoor sports, including biking, mountaineering, skiing, backpacking, and camping, has coverage of major sporting events, reviews of equipment, current sports news, and vacation guides. The "News in Review" has past top stories, special reports, and event coverage.

SPORTSLINE USA

http://www.sportsline.com/index.html

SportsLine has the latest news and updates on all professional sports. The "Sports Menu" allows you to choose a sport, such as baseball, auto racing, golf, the Olympics, skiing, and others. The "Odds and Ends" page has analyses of scores. The "Newsroom" has columns, photos, news, and a search engine.

 # TRAVEL

CITYNET

http://www.city.net

CityNet offers information about travel, entertainment, business, government, and community services for more than two thousand cities worldwide.

VIRTUAL TOURIST

http://www.vtourist.com

This site offers map-based links to local servers throughout the world. If you want to view Web sites in Fiji, Bermuda, or wherever, you can find them via Virtual Tourist.

WORLD FACT BOOK

http://www.odci.gov/cia/publications/factbook/index.html

Produced by the Central Intelligence Agency, the World Fact Book has information on geography, climates, the environment, customs, economics, legal systems, and communications for nearly every county in the world.

WOMEN'S STUDIES

THE WOMEN'S RESOURCE PROJECT

http://sunsite.unc.edu/cheryb/women

The Women's Resource Project has a "Library Resources" page that links you to libraries on the Net that have women's studies collections. Connection to a Women's Studies Listserv is provided along with links to university women's programs and women's resources on the Internet.

WOMEN'S STUDIES DATABASE

http://www.inform.umd.edu:8080/EdRes/Topic/WomensStudies

This large database collection of women's studies and general women's issues has a search engine that searches the entire directory by keywords. Major directories include announcements, bibliographies, calls for papers, employment, government and politics, classic texts, references, and syllabi from universities. Other gopher and Web sites about women's issues also are given.

CHAPTER 6

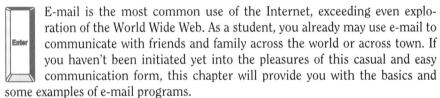

E-Mail, Listservs, and Usenet Newsgroups

E-mail is the most common use of the Internet, exceeding even exploration of the World Wide Web. As a student, you already may use e-mail to communicate with friends and family across the world or across town. If you haven't been initiated yet into the pleasures of this casual and easy communication form, this chapter will provide you with the basics and some examples of e-mail programs.

Increasingly, e-mail is becoming part of the college classroom. Your instructor may have you submit assignments by e-mail or may suggest that you use it as an alternative way to communicate with him or her. You may find it easier to ask your instructor questions by e-mail than you do in class or in an office visit. You also may have a class mailing list or Listserv that you use as a forum for discussion of topics related to your classroom studies.

This chapter discusses and demonstrates the basics of e-mail, Listservs, and Usenet newsgroups. Listservs are mailing lists that you subscribe to, and you receive messages in your e-mail box from members. Usenet, though not accessed by e-mail, is included in this chapter because it provides communication possibilities similar to Listservs. You do not subscribe to Usenet newsgroups; rather, you access them through a news reader such as the ones included in Netscape Communicator and Internet Explorer.

In addition to class Listservs or newsgroups, you can use public groups as additional avenues for research. This chapter will suggest how to find groups discussing topics relevant to your class research. These groups may include other students or professionals in related fields. When you locate a group that seems relevant, it is a good idea to observe the group discussion for several days before you participate. This is called "lurking." After a few days of reading other people's postings, you will have a good idea of how to participate in the discussion. You may ask, for example, for suggestions about Web sites, magazine articles, or books that are particularly relevant to your topic. Or you may find that the group offers opinions you can quote in your research paper. Be aware, however, that information posted in Listservs and newsgroups generally is opinion, not verifiable fact.

 ## ANATOMY OF AN E-MAIL

An e-mail address looks something like this:

login@serveraddress

An example would be **john@unm.edu** if John is a student at the University of New Mexico. Or, if John has his e-mail account on a commercial server, his address could look like this:

johnj@instantnet.com.

Thus, all e-mail addresses consist of two parts, the individual's log-in name and the server address. Often the log-in name is some version of the person's real name. The server address may end in **.edu** if the e-mail account is on a university-owned server. Commercial servers generally have **.com** or **.net** endings to their addresses.

When you obtain your e-mail address, you likely will have some choice about a log-in name. Choose a contracted version of your name that will be easy to remember, both for your memory's sake and for friends who may want to send you mail. Your log-in name also may be required to log in to your university's e-mail server, and you probably will be asked to declare a password to protect your account.

 ## E-MAIL PROGRAMS

Through many university systems, you can access your e-mail through your Web browser. The following brief discussion tells how to use e-mail programs through Netscape Navigator and Internet Explorer. Also included is a brief discussion of Pine, an older e-mail program many universities use. If you do not have access to one of these three programs, however, your e-mail program will function in a similar fashion.

NETSCAPE MAIL

The e-mail program included in Netscape Communicator is popular because you can read your mail without leaving your Web browser. From the *Communicator* pull-down menu, select *Messenger Mailbox*, and you will see a display similar to this one:

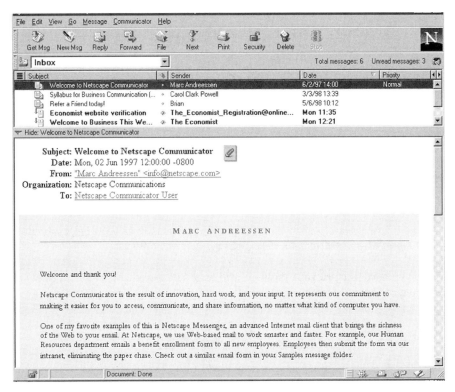

The example shows a list of messages in the *Inbox*. You may need to click on *Get Msg* to download your new messages from the server. If you have not provided your e-mail address and server address, you may need to do so through the *Preferences* option on the *Edit* menu. Otherwise, the browser does not know where to find your e-mail. (*Note*: if you are using Netscape in one of your school's labs, you may need to remove your e-mail address when you are finished. Otherwise someone else could send e-mail from your mailbox.)

Highlight the message you want to read, and it will be displayed in the lower window. When you have read a message, you can delete it by clicking on *Delete*. You can also *Reply*, *Forward*, *Print*, or *File* your message by clicking on the appropriate icon. If you want to send a message, click on *New Msg*, and you will see a box where you can enter an e-mail address, a subject line, and type your message.

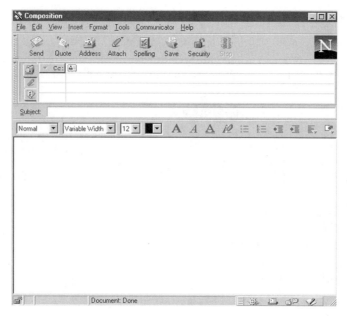

When you have finished your message, you can spell check by clicking on *Spelling* and then send your message by clicking *Send*. At any time, you can get help or learn more about Netscape Mail features by selecting an option from the *Help* menu.

INTERNET EXPLORER OUTLOOK EXPRESS

Like Netscape Mail, you can read your e-mail in Internet Explorer without leaving the browser. Outlook Express is one of several programs that allow you to do so. If you want to read your mail, click on the *Mail* icon on the Explorer screen, and choose *Read Mail*. You will see a screen similar to this one:

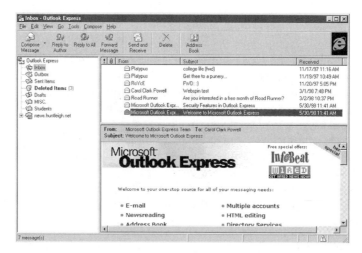

Your e-mail messages will be listed in the upper-right box. You may need to click on *Send and Receive* to download current messages. If you do not have an e-mail or server address indicated in the browser preferences, you may need to specify one, so the browser knows where to locate your e-mail. If you are not prompted by the program, go to the *Tools* menu and select *Accounts*. (*Note*: if you are using Explorer Outlook Express in one of your school's labs, you may need to remove your e-mail address when you are finished. Otherwise someone else could send e-mail from your mailbox.) Highlight one of your messages by clicking on it, and it will be displayed in the lower right box. After you read, you can delete the highlighted message by clicking *Delete*. You also can save the message in one of your folders listed in the box on the left of the screen. Drag a highlighted message until it merges with the folder you select. You can add folders to organize your saved e-mail by going to the *File* menu and selecting *Folder*.

If you want to create a message, click on *Compose Message* (or select it from the Explorer main screen by clicking on *Mail* and choosing *New Message*). The template provides you with spaces for the recipient's e-mail address, any addresses for duplicate copies, a subject line, and attachments. Compose your message in the large box in the lower portion of the screen. When you have finished, you can check your spelling by going to the *Tools* menu. Send your message by clicking *Send*.

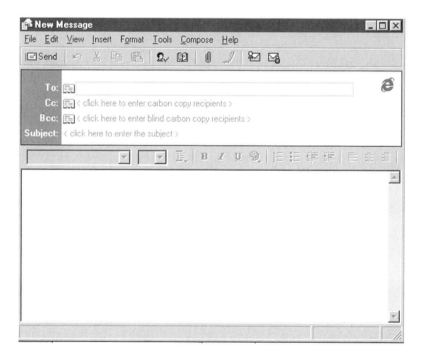

Outlook Express has many more features you can use to enhance your e-mail communication. Learn about them by exploring the information available through the *Help* menu.

PINE

An older but efficient e-mail program, Pine is used by many colleges and community organizations that offer text-only access to the Internet. Typically, you access Pine through a menu option when you dial your university's Internet number, or you may Telnet to it (information Telnet allows you to log in to a remote computer network and use its programs). Ask your lab assistant or instructor how to connect to Pine if that is the program available. You will be asked for your log-on information (e-mail address) and a password. Then you will see a welcome screen something like this:

```
?       HELP              -   Get help using Pine

C       COMPOSE MESSAGE   -   Compose and send a message

I       FOLDER INDEX      -   View messages in current folder

L       FOLDER LIST       -   Select a folder to view

A       ADDRESS BOOK      -   update address book

S       SETUP             -   Configure or update Pine

Q       QUIT              -   Exit the Pine program
```

Pine is a menu-driven program with clearly displayed commands and shortcut keys. To compose a message, for example, use your arrow keys to highlight *Compose Message* and press *Enter*. You will see a screen where you can write your e-mail message.

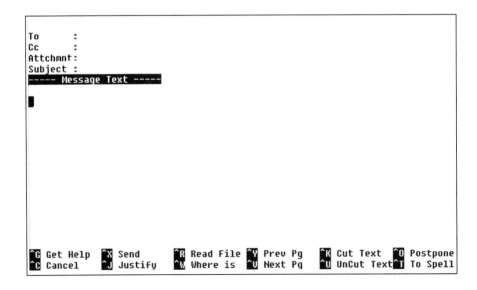

```
To      :
Cc      :
Attchmnt:
Subject :
----- Message Text -----
█



^G Get Help  ^X Send    ^R Read File  ^Y Prev Pg  ^K Cut Text   ^O Postpone
^C Cancel    ^J Justify ^W Where is   ^V Next Pg  ^U UnCut Text ^T To Spell
```

Notice the list of commands across the bottom of the screen. You can use them to print, spell check, and so forth. To save, for example, press *Control-S*.

To read your mail, select *Folder List* from the opening menu, and press *Enter*. You will see a folder called *Inbox*. Highlight it, and press *Enter* again. You will see a list of your e-mail messages if you have received any. Highlight the e-mail message you want to read, press *Enter*, and you will see the message displayed.

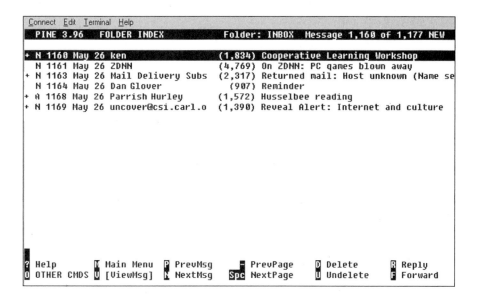

 # GROUP DISCUSSION VIA E-MAIL AND USENET NEWSGROUPS

Thousands of people communicate every day with others of like interests through two types of discussion groups on the Internet: e-mail discussion groups and newsgroups. The general format of both types is the same. One person sends a message (you can also call it a *posting*) about a topic, which you can identify by the message's subject line. Other people respond about that topic, using the same or similar subject lines and giving their own viewpoint or information. This generates a discussion *thread* or group of posting about the same topic. Threads may last days, weeks, or years, and one discussion group may have numerous threads going at the same time.

You subscribe to e-mail discussion groups, and the postings come to your mailbox. You access newsgroups differently, by connecting to a part of your server that stores the postings of newsgroups. Newsgroups (which may not have anything to do with news or current events) are also called Usenet newsgroups. Both types of discussion groups predate the World Wide Web, though you can access them now through the Web with either Netscape or Explorer. You also can access both types in other ways. Any e-mail program will serve just as well for e-mail discussion groups, and other newsgroup readers are available that do not access newsgroups through the Web.

E-MAIL DISCUSSION GROUPS (ALSO CALLED LISTSERVS OR MAILING LISTS)

Whether you are interested in discussing current events, accounting for small businesses, or freedom of speech, an e-mail discussion group (sometimes called Listservs or mailing lists) probably exists that matches your interests. Some groups require members to meet certain criteria, such as membership in a college class or having a certain type of degree, but the majority of groups are open to the public. You subscribe to an e-mail discussion group by sending a message to an address managed by an automated program (usually Listserv, Majordomo, or Listproc). Generally, the program subscribes you to the list, sends you a welcome message, and then you begin receiving the group's discussion in the form of e-mail messages members post.

Subscribe and Unsubscribe Commands

Commands such as *subscribe* or *unsubscribe* are sent directly to the list server. Usually that address looks something like this:

> listserv@domainname

Listserv-type programs are generally case insensitive, which means you can type *Listserv* or *listserv* and the program will respond to either. If the Listserv address is **listserv@xuniversity.edum**, you would put that address on the *To*: line of your e-mail message. Other Listserv programs have addresses similar to **majordomo@xcompany.com** or **listname-request@xcompany.com**. Use whatever address you have been given for the group. Leave the subject line blank.

In the message body, you will need to give a subscribe command. These vary slightly depending on which Listserv program the server is running, but generally they follow this format:

> *Subscribe command*: subscribe [listname] [firstname lastname]

> *Unsubscribe command*: unsubscribe [listname]

For example, if you were subscribing to a Listproc discussion group called apple-1, your message might read

> subscribe apple-1 James Moffit

After the automated program receives your request for subscription, you will receive a message informing you of commands to use and other information the group wishes subscribers to have. It is a good idea to save this message, for you may want to refer to it later.

Posting Messages to a Group

To post, you send your message to an entirely different address than the one you used to subscribe. Usually the address looks like this:

listname@domainname

You will find the posting address among the directions in your welcome message from the group. Do include a subject line, for many participants may decide whether or not to read a message from what the subject line indicates about the message.

Finding Interesting Groups

Several Web sites now offer searchable lists of e-mail discussion groups. Connect to one of these sites, and follow the directions for using its search features to find groups in your area of interest:

CataList
http://www.lsoft.com/lists/listref.html
Liszt
http://www.liszt.com/
Directory of Scholarly Electronic Conferences
http://www.lib.ncsu.edu/reference-acadlists.html
Publically Accessible Mailing Lists
http://www.neosoft.com/internet/paml

You also can do an e-mail keyword search for a group focusing on a particular topic. Send a message to listserv@listserv.net (or another Listserv maintaining a list of Listservs) including the keywords. The message would look like this:

list global [keywords]

If, for example, you were interested in a group discussing campus conditions, you might use the message **list global campus**. You would receive a list of e-mail discussion groups with that keyword, and the list would look something like this:

```
CAMPCLIM            CAMPCLIM@UAFSYSB.UARK.EDU
                    Campus Climate

CAMPCOM             CAMPCOM@ASUVM.INRE.ASU.EDU
                    CAMPCOM - Campus Communities List

CAMPUS-LIFE         CAMPUS-LIFE@LISTSERV.AOL.COM
                    Newsletter for Campus Life magazine online.

CAMPUSCARE-L        CAMPUSCARE-L@POSTOFFICE.CSO.UIUC.EDU
                    campus environments for children

CAMPUSDIR-L         CAMPUSDIR-L@TC.UMN.EDU
                    CampusDir-1: Campus Directors Discussion List

CAMPUSGS            CAMPUSGS@LISTSERV.TAMU.EDU
                    Campus Girl Scouts Mailing List

CAMPUS_CRUSAD...    CAMPUS_CRUSADE_FOR_CHRIST@LISTSERV.VT.EDU
                    Campus_Crusade_for_Christ secondary mailing List

CAMPUS_LIGHT        CAMLIGHT@WVNVM.WVNET.EDU
                    Campus Light

CCAT                CCAT@LISTSERV.UIC.EDU
                    Chicago Campus Advisory Team

CCBAY-L             CCBAY-L@UCBCMSA.BITNET
                    CCBAY-L - Campus Coalition for Human Rights and Social Justice

CCC                 CCC@LIST.UVM.EDU
                    Campus-wide Communications Committee

CCC_VT              CCC_VT@LISTSERV.VT.EDU
                    Campus Crusade for Christ at Virginia Tech Mailing List

CCN                 CCN@ASU.EDU
                    Campus Computing News
```

USENET NEWSGROUPS

Though the function of Usenet newsgroups is similar in many ways to Listservs, they vary in how you access them. As noted earlier, you subscribe to Listservs, and the messages come to your mailbox. Newsgroup messages, in contrast, are collected at a central location. You connect to a particular group your Internet provider has subscribed to and read selected messages. An advantage of newsgroups is that the messages are never downloaded to your e-mail, so they do not clog your in-box. On the other hand, you have to develop the habit of checking your group messages, or you do not get the benefits of participating in a group discussion.

Newsgroups are broken into categories that are indicated by a prefix to the name of the group. The most common prefixes are

alt   alternative—broad range of topics
biz   business

comp	computers, computer science
misc	other
news	news about newsgroups
rec	recreation and hobbies
sci	scientific
soc	social issues
talk	debate

The prefix is followed by one or more specific subject names. For example, **news.newusers.questions** is a group that answers questions from new participants in newsgroups.

Reading Newsgroups in Netscape

In Netscape you access Usenet newsgroups by clicking on the Message Center bar on the component bar that is usually in the bottom right of your screen. The Collabra Discussion Groups (Netscape's name for newsgroups) icon is the second from the right.

Alternatively, you can go to the *Communicator* menu at the top of your Netscape screen and select *Collabra Discussion Groups*.

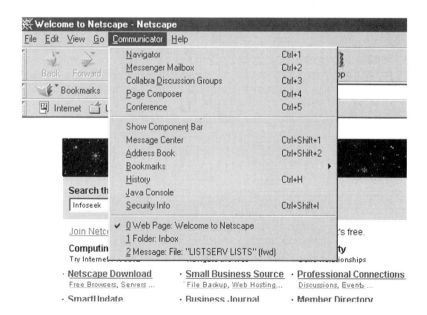

You will receive this Message Center screen, which displays the newsgroups you are subscribed to and also provides a link to your e-mail box:

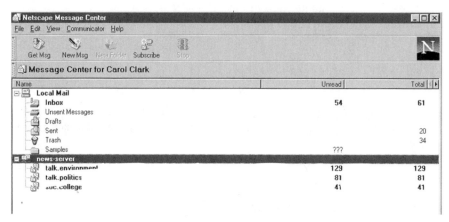

Your lab may have subscribed to some standard groups for you. If you want to add additional groups, or if you have none displayed, click on the *Subscribe* icon. A list of groups will appear, and you can select those that look interesting. Or you can select the tab on the subscribe screen labeled *Search for a Group*, and you will see a screen like this one:

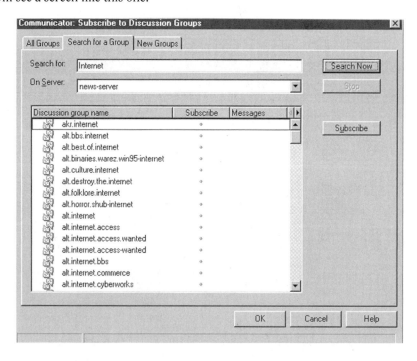

In the box at the top of the screen, you can enter a word for a keyword search of the groups available. In this case, *Internet* is entered, and the screen below displays the groups with the word *Internet* in their names.

Click on the name of a subscribed group, and you will see a screen that displays a list of the group's postings. Here the group is *talk.environment*.

Next to some of the items, you will see icons that look like small spools of thread and a plus sign. These stand for *threads*, or linked messages all discussing the same topic. Click on the plus sign and see a list of messages in that thread. Click on any of the messages on the list, and the text will be displayed in the box below. The message displayed from the group *talk.environment* relates to the banning of Jet Skis.

If you are reading a posting to Usenet and want to reply, you have the choice of replying only to the writer of the posting. Or you can post to the group. Click on *Reply*, and a dialog box will inquire whether you want to reply to the individual, the group, or the group and the individual. Choose an option, and you will receive a box where you can type your posting.

Reading Newsgroups in Internet Explorer

To access Usenet newsgroups in Internet Explorer, go the *Mail* menu and select *Read News*.

If you are using Microsoft Outlook as your newsgroup reader, your screen will appear like the one here. If you are using another news reader with Internet Explorer, the configuration will be somewhat different, but it will offer the same capabilities.

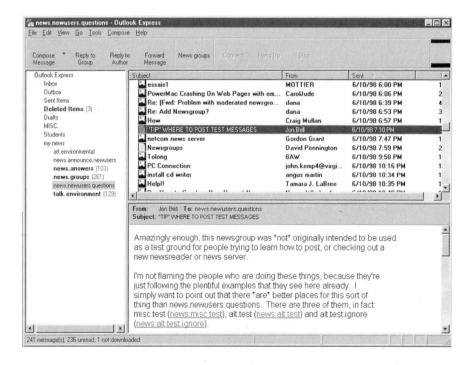

In the box on the right side, which also offers links to e-mail, you will find listed the newsgroups you are subscribed to. If you click on the name of one of the groups, it will display a list of unread messages in the top right box. Click on a message, and it will appear in the lower right box. In this example, the group *news.newusers.questions* is highlighted, a group where you can post questions about newsgroups. The message displayed in the bottom-right box discusses other groups that are appropriate for posting test messages.

If you have no groups listed in the box on the right of the screen or if you want to subscribe to additional groups, click on *News groups*. You will receive this box, where you can review Usenet newsgroups your provider has subscribed to:

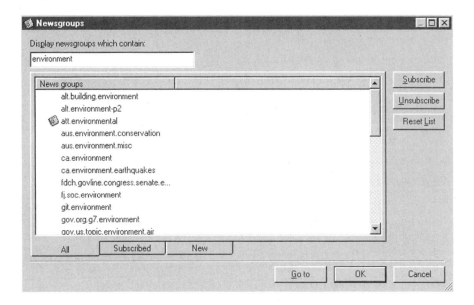

You can type in a keyword in the box, and Outlook Express will list the groups that include that keyword in the name of their group. In the screen illustrated, the word *environment* was entered, and groups are listed that include that word. Note that one group, *alt.environment*, has an icon next to it. That means the user has subscribed to the group.

When you have a group selected and you want to post a message to it, click on *Reply to Group*. If you want to send a message only to the author of the message you have been reading, click on *Reply to Author*. In either case, you will receive a box where you can type your message; then click on *Send*, which you will find in the *File* menu.

Finding Relevant Groups

As described previously, news-reading software such as Internet Explorer and Netscape Navigator have a keyword search function that can be used to find groups, but this will not work for groups that use abbreviations for their names. Try a keyword search at one of the sources for group archives, such as DejaNews (http://www.dejanews.com). You can locate the name of a group in the archives and then access newsgroups through your browser and read what is going on currently with the same group.

CHAPTER 7

Documenting Internet Sources

To use the extensive resource materials available on the World Wide Web in research projects, you must document your sources. This allows your audience, should they be interested, to retrace your research steps and look at the materials you have used. To do this, you need to provide references in the text to the materials you have used and at the end of your paper furnish a works-cited or reference page. Be aware, however, that Web addresses change and sources sometimes disappear. It is advisable to print out or save on disk any reference material crucial to your research. You can, thus, continually refer to the material, and you can, if necessary, provide a copy for your instructor.

Because the use of Internet sources has grown so quickly, conventions for documenting Web sources are still developing. Check with your professor first about his or her preferences for documenting online sources. You may find handbooks or sites on the Web that suggest somewhat different approaches to documentation of Web sources. This chapter offers models for citing sources that are consistent with Modern Language Association (MLA) and American Psychological Association (APA) styles.

→ MODERN LANGUAGE ASSOCIATION STYLE

For MLA style, also refer to the *MLA Handbook for Writers of Research Papers* and the MLA Web site, http://www.mla.org/set_stl.htm.

IN-TEXT CITATION

Modern Language Association style uses parenthetical (in-text) references that are keyed to a works-cited page at the end of the paper. For print sources, the name of the author and the page number provide the references. This type of citation is difficult for Web sources because few have page numbers, and many do not have specified authors. If you have an author and page or section number, give them. If no author is specified, use a shortened part of the title of the text.

EXAMPLE ➡

According to an *Internet World* article, "Job Trak, the nation's leading online job listing service, claims to have already been used by more than a million students and alumni, with more than 150,000 employers and 300 college career centers posting new jobs daily" (Grusky).

WORKS-CITED PAGE

Ideally, a works-cited page provides sufficient information about all the sources you have used so that your readers can locate the materials should they wish to do so. For Web sources, pages change or disappear; thus, you need to include the date you accessed the site in addition to any publication date the source specified.

These are some examples of typical documents you might need to reference:

1. An online text with a print equivalent:
Give the information for the print version first, then the publisher of the online version, the date accessed, and the Web address.

Reilly, Bernard F., *Library of Congress Prints and Photographs: An Illustrated Guide.* Washington: Library of Congress, 1995. Library of Congress. 22 July 1998. <http://www.loc.gov/rr/rarebook/guide/toc.html>.

2. An article in an online magazine without a print equivalent:
Give both the date of publication and the date of access.

Baird, Sara. "Mom's a Head-Banger." *Salon*. 7 Oct. 1977. 21 Oct. 1997. <http://www.salonmagazine.com/mwt/feature/1997/10/07rock.html>.

3. Professional Web site:
Virtual Computer Library. U of Texas. 20 June 1998. <http://www.utexas.edu/computer/vcl>.

3. Personal Web site:
Barlow, John Perry. Home page. 4 July 1998. <http://www.eff.org/~barlow>.

4. E-mail:
Walker, Judith. E-mail to Doug Lauren. 14 April 1998.

AMERICAN PSYCHOLOGICAL ASSOCIATION STYLE

For APA style also refer to the *Publication Manual of the American Psychological Association* and the APA Web site, http://www.apa.org/journals/webref.html.

IN-TEXT CITATIONS

American Psychological Association style specifies giving the author and date after the referenced material in the text. This type of citation is difficult for Web sources, because many texts do not have specified authors or dates of publication. If you have an author and date of publication, give them. If no author is specified, use a shortened part of the title of the text.

EXAMPLE ➡

According to an *Internet World* article, "Job Trak, the nation's leading online job listing service, claims to have already been used by more than a million students and alumni, with more than 150,000 employers and 300 college career centers posting new jobs daily" (Grusky, 1996).

The APA also suggests citing Web site home pages by giving the address in the text (e.g., **http://www.apa.org**). No citation on the reference page is needed. The same is true of e-mail: Cite it in the text but not in the reference list. For example, an in-text citation might look like this: "James A. Smith (personal communication, March 18, 1998)." For specific articles posted on the World Wide Web, always cite the article in the reference list and include "retrieved from" and the date.

REFERENCE LIST

Instead of a works-cited page, APA specifies a reference list. Since you can cite Web page addresses in the text, according to the APA Web page, you would put Web references in the reference list only if they refer to specific articles or books published on the World Wide Web.

EXAMPLES ➡

American Psychological Association. *How to Cite Information from the World Wide Web.* [FAQ posted on the World Wide Web]. Retrieved July 25, 1998 from the World Wide Web: http://www.apa.org/journals/webref.html

Kraut, R., & Lundmark, V. (1998). Internet Paradox: A Social Technology That Reduces Social Involvement and Psychological Well-Being? *American Psychologist, 53,* 1017–1031. Retrieved from the World Wide Web: http://www.apa.org/journals/amp/amp5391017.html

Working the Web

Part III

CREATING WEB PAGES

III Creating Web Pages

WORKING
THE
WEB

CHAPTER 8

The Basics of Creating Web Pages

The World Wide Web offers students a unique set of publishing opportunities. For the first time in history, students (and other individuals)
can publish texts, graphics, videos, and sound documents for a potential worldwide audience. If someone in Australia or Sweden knows your
address or is simply browsing student pages at your university, he or
she can view your work. No longer are the essays or other texts you write restricted to an audience of classmates, professors, or even other students at
your university.

Many students at various schools and grade levels have published their own
sets of pages on the World Wide Web. The level of quality varies widely according to the author's purpose, talent, and level of interest. Some want simply to
introduce themselves to the world with some personal information, a picture,
or perhaps some of their poetry or short stories. These authors often include
links to favorite sites or a copy of a résumé. Such pages may be simple and
charming, as is the home page on p. 116 authored by Christine Bishop. Her
page clearly and attractively organizes her links to personal data, to class essays,
and to a photo gallery.

Or they may display original art and poetry, as does Hans Neseth's Web site.
His home page is reproduced on p. 116.

Other students choose to do theme-centered pages, perhaps about a topic related to their majors or other personal interests, such as Katherine Hughes's Dark
Elegy site, which was also featured in Chapter 3. The site commemorates a sculpture that is a memorial for those who died in an airplane bombing, including a
number of students from Syracuse University.

You, too, can create your own set of Web pages, and they can be as simple or
as complex as you desire. You may want to begin with a modest project, perhaps
three or four pages with an interesting background pattern and a few photos.

Christine Bishop's home page.

Hans Neseth's home page.

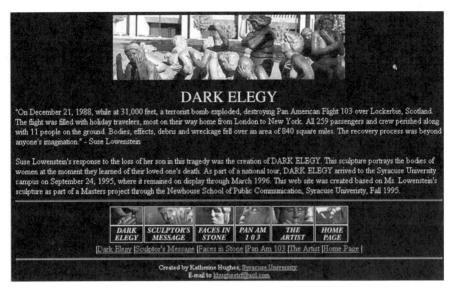

Katherine Hughes's home page.

Then, as your knowledge of Web page design increases, you may find yourself authoring more ambitious projects.

To create Web pages you need to use Hypertext markup language (HTML), the tag language used to tell Web browsers how to display the contents of your pages. If you learn the basics of HTML, you will have an idea of how the language works for page construction. Then, you can either learn the intricacies of HTML, and construct your pages using that language, or you may decide to use one of the many editors that, like word processing programs, allow you to create a sophisticated look without actually doing the coding yourself. Some Web page experts do both. They use an editor to generate the bulk of their pages but use their in-depth knowledge of HTML to add refinements to their pages. This chapter of *Working the Web* introduces you both to HTML and to an editor built into Netscape Navigator.

 # HYPERTEXT MARKUP LANGUAGE

HTML uses a system of codes to tag various parts of a World Wide Web document. These *tags* determine how each part of the final document is displayed when viewed with a Web browser. At first glance, HTML documents may seem difficult to understand. Unlike many word processing programs, HTML documents do not provide the luxury of "What You See Is What You Get" (WYSIWYG) during creation. Instead, you insert codes, or tags, into the document that indicate paragraphs, bold type, and so on. A Web browser interprets these codes as instructions.

As an illustration of HTML, take a look at this test page in HTML as viewed in a text editor program, below, and as viewed through Netscape, p.119.

As you can see, even in this very simple document, the HTML looks different from the version a Web browser produced. The heading at the top of the document, for example, appears in large type in the Netscape version but not in the HTML version. But why not have a WYSIWYG convention for HTML? It works fine for WordPerfect, Microsoft Word, Claris Works, and many other word processing programs. The problem with a WYSIWYG system for HTML is that HTML documents are viewed by a variety of Web browsers and each will display the HTML document in a slightly different way. In fact, two users may have the same version of the same browser and the document display still will vary depending on the differences between the preferences each user has set in the browser. Because of user preferences and differences between browsers, the rules and tags of HTML allow for the differences in display that may arise from machine to machine.

HTML files are written in plain text, which means they do not have embedded word processing codes. Therefore, an HTML document is constructed with a text-editing program that does not create its own embedded codes. A regular word

---

SAMPLE HTML DOCUMENT VIEWED IN TEXT EDITOR

```
<html>

<head>

<title> HTML Defined</title>

</head>

<body>

<font size = + 3> Hypertext Markup Language Defined </font>
```

Hypertext markup language (HTML) is a system of codes that, when embedded in documents, are understood by World Wide Web browser programs to indicate the structure of Web pages. The language is hypertext because one page such as this can have a link to <A HREF://webaddress> another page </A>. A reader simply clicks on the highlighted text to connect to the second page.

```
</body>

</html>
```

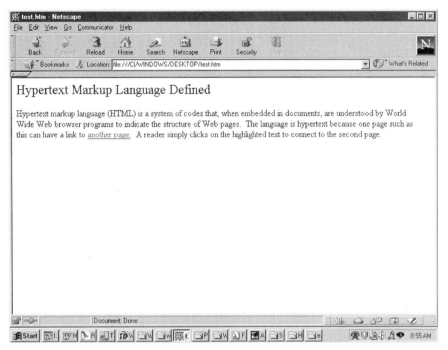

A sample HTML document viewed in Netscape. Copyright © 1999 Netscape Communications Corp. All Rights Reserved. This page may not be reprinted or copied without the express permission of Netscape.

processor may be used to write HTML pages; however, the document must be saved in a text-only format that eliminates the embedded word processing codes. Also, recent versions of word processing programs may offer the option of saving a text file as an HTML document. *Note: When creating an HTML document, your file name must have the extension* .htm *or* .html so that Web browsers can read the file.

HTML is white-space insensitive. When a browser displays an HTML document, all of that document's on-screen formatting is determined by the tags and containers that surround that document's content. Any extra spaces, empty lines, or other blank areas in the document have no effect on its final layout when viewed with a browser. Therefore, while some extra spaces or empty lines may make it easier to read an HTML document while editing it, those spaces will not matter when viewing the document with a Web browser. Every space, no matter how large, will be interpreted simply as a single space. A tag must be used to create spaces larger than one character or to put in breaks between lines or paragraphs.

HTML documents are made up of four distinct parts: content, tags, links, and in-line media.

▼ The *content* of an HTML document is the text users can read and interact with.

▼ *Tags* are the parts of an HTML document end users do not directly see, but they shape how the content is displayed.

▼ *Links* are the part of an HTML document that connect one document to another or one part of a document to another part of the same document.

▼ *In-line media* refers to any other media, most commonly graphics, the browser displays as part of an HTML document.

 # TAGS

The first step involved in learning to create HTML documents is to study how tags shape and organize a document. HTML tags are set apart from a document's content with angle brackets (<>). The tags are not case sensitive so the tag <HTML> and the tag <html> are the same. They often occur in pairs, one tag at the beginning and one tag at the end of the content they affect. The closing tag always is preceded with a slash (/). These tag pairs define areas called *containers*. Any content within a container must obey the rules set down by the tags that define that container. For example, content inside a boldface container will be displayed as bold text by the browser.

<HTML>

The HTML tags always should be the first and last tags in an HTML document. These are the tags that tell the browser where the HTML document begins and ends, and they look like this:

    <html>

    </html>

The absolutely simplest Web page would contain nothing but these two tags. When viewed with a browser, this would display a blank page.

<HEAD> AND <BODY>

The head and body container sets divide the document into two sections. The top section of the document is called the *head*. The tags for the head are simply these:

    <head>

    </head>

The most common and simplest element that resides in the head section of an HTML document is the title. The title container is delineated by these tags:

<title>

</title>

Any content put into the title container is displayed in the title bar (above the buttons) of some browser windows. The title is not part of the text displayed in the browser's display window.

The title also has a couple of other uses. It is the reference used in the history list in the browser, and if the user makes a bookmark pointing to an HTML document, the title becomes the name for that bookmark. The title element is even important during the cataloging of Web pages. World Wide Web search engines search the Web, cataloging pages according to their title elements. If essential information about the document is not included in the title element, the document will not be indexed accurately by any search engine that examines it.

The second section of the document resides in the body container. The tags for the body follow:

<body>

</body>

Between the body tags lies all of the content that actually get displayed in the browser. All of the text, links, pictures, and other in-line media are contained within the body tags.

Line breaks indicate the start of a new line. Remember that Web browsers will ignore any extra spaces inserted into an HTML document. They also will ignore any line breaks in the HTML document not marked by the <br> tag. The <br> tag does not form a container but is simply inserted where a line break is desired. So, when viewing a document whose source HTML contains the following example, the browser will only insert line breaks where the <br> tags have been placed.

EXAMPLE ➡

Hypertext markup language is made up of elements, including the following:

Head

Body

Graphic

<P>

Paragraph tags tell the browser to indicate a paragraph break by skipping a line. Like the <br> tag, the paragraph tag does not form a container but is placed where a paragraph break is desired. In the following example, a browser would display all of the text in one block and would skip a line when it interpreted the <p> tag.

EXAMPLE ➡

Hypertext markup language is a system of codes that, when embedded in documents, are understood by World Wide Web browser programs to indicate the structure of Web pages.

<p>

<HR>

This code generates a horizontal rule that tells the browser to create a long line stretching across the display window. A horizontal rule can be used to break text into sections or to draw the reader's attention to a particular part of a Web document. Like the <br> and <p> tags, the <hr> tag is used without a closing tag to indicate where in the content the horizontal rule is to appear. In this example, the heading would appear with a horizontal rule above and below.

EXAMPLE ➡

<hr>

<h1> HTML Defined </h1>

<hr>

 # ANCHORS

The hypertext nature of the World Wide Web means that individual documents can be linked together. In an HTML document these links are formed with anchor tags. *Anchors* may connect to other parts of a single HTML document, to other pages in the same group of documents, or to documents created by a different author on the other side of the globe

The general format for an anchor follows:

<a href = "URL address"> Content </a>

The <a tag indicates an anchor, and href (hypertext reference) refers to a Web page address. This tells the browser it should highlight the words given in the anchor's content area and make them a hot link. If the user clicks on the highlighted words, the browser will retrieve the document indicated by the anchor's URL address between quote marks (remember that URL stands for Uniform Resource Locator and that it is the standard way of expressing the location of any information available through the Internet). The </a> tag at the end closes the anchor container.

For example, the English Department home page at the Web site for the university where I teach (reproduced below) has a link to the university's home page. You can tell that the text "The University of Texas at El Paso" is a hot link because it is highlighted. When you place your cursor on it, a URL address appears in the lower left-hand portion of the browser screen.

In the HTML document for the page, the anchor includes the URL of the Web page to be linked. It looks like this:

<a href="http://www.utep.edu">The University of Texas at El Paso</a>

The <a href= "http://www.utep.edu"> portion turns the words that follow, *The University of Texas at El Paso*, into a hot link to the university's home page. Finally, the </a> code ends the hot link.

The University of Texas at El Paso
Department of English
113 Hudspeth Hall
(915)747-5731

●CHAIRPERSON: Tony Jason Stafford

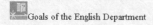Goals of the English Department

The English Department is dedicated to excellent teaching, where English majors/minors have the opportunity to receive ongoing personal attention as they develop critical and creative thinking skills while maturing as careful readers and effective writers.

The hypertext link, "The University of Texas at El Paso," appears in blue and is underlined.

SOME CONSIDERATIONS FOR LINKED PAGES

▼ When you provide hot links in a page, it is preferable to make the words for the link part of your sentence structure. Do not say "click here to see the Grand Canyon"; rather, say "**The Grand Canyon** offers spectacular views," with *Grand Canyon* as the hot link.

▼ Make the link a few words, not one word or a whole sentence. *Grand Canyon* in the above example is about the right length. If you highlighted the whole sentence, "**The Grand Canyon offers spectacular views,**" it distracts from your text.

▼ Remember that every linked page your viewers select has waiting time as the page downloads. Try to give some subtle clues in your text about what readers can expect at the linked page so that they can judge if they want to wait while the page loads.

 # IMAGES

Images are the most common form of in-line media on the Web. Video and sound media also can be part of HTML documents, though they are beyond the scope of this book. In-line image tags allow an author to include photos, drawings, icons, colored bars, and other pictorial supplements intermixed with the text of the HTML document. The basic form of the in-line image tag is <img scr= "image.format">, with the IMG SRC standing for *image source*.

EXAMPLE ➡

<img src="photo 1.gif">

The <img src="..."> tag indicates the link to the image source. Generally, the image file is placed in the same file directory on the host server as the HTML document. When a Web browser reads the page, the image is called up and displayed automatically.

Images can be placed almost anywhere in the body of an HTML document. They can be between paragraphs, within paragraphs, in a list of items, or even used as all or part of a heading.

Many students create their own images by scanning photos or graphics. Graphics of various kinds also are available in collections on the World Wide Web (see Chapter 10). The basics of the scanning process are fairly simple, though they vary from one scanning program to another. See Chapter 10 for basic instruction, and consult the help desk in the lab or wherever the scanner is located for instructions on how to scan and save images. For now, the most widely recognized format for in-line images on the Web is GIF. GIF stands for Graphic Interchange Format, and all graphical browsers will recognize and display images in GIF format. They also support JPEG or JPG (Joint Photographic Experts Group) images.

It is also possible to make an image into a hypertext link. The tag for an image link should look like this:

```
<a href="URL"><img src="image.gif"></a>
```

TEXT ALTERNATIVES TO IMAGES

Browsers that cannot support images will display the word *IMAGE* in place of the graphic. If you would prefer instead that text-based browsers such as Lynx display descriptive text instead of the world *IMAGE*, you can provide an alternative. The descriptive text is used as an add-on to the in-line image tag with the addition of the worked code "alt" for alternative:

```
<img src="photo1.gif" alt="Logo">
```

INCLUDING YOUR E-MAIL ADDRESS

It is customary to include address information at the end of your home page document. Enclose your name, e-mail address, and other information you want to include within the address tags <address> and </address>. If you want to give a hot link to your e-mail address, use this source code:

```
<a href=mailto:yourlogin@yourschool.edu>
yourlogin@yourschool.edu</a>.
```

The first part, <a href=mailto:yourlogin@yourschool.edu>, is the hypertext link. The second part, yourlogin@yourschool.edu</a>, is the anchor, the text that actually appears on your page. The text is followed by the </a> code which ends the anchor.

If your e-mail address were jsmith@xuniversity.edu, the code for the link to your e-mail address would look like this example.

EXAMPLE ➡

```
<a href=mailto:jsmith@xuniversity.edu> jsmith@xuniversity.edu</a>.
```

BASIC HTML COMMANDS

<html> </html>

Placed at beginning and end of document

<head> </head>

Indicates header information

<title> </title>

Title (appears in browser header, not in body of page)

<body> </body>

Encloses the body of the HTML document

<Address> </Address>

Encloses the address information

PARAGRAPHS AND BREAKS

<p>

Blank line (indicates paragraphs)

(continued)

 # WRITING A TEST WEB PAGE

Before you can begin writing interesting and sophisticated World Wide Web pages, you must begin with the basics. Practice by creating a test document with a text editor, and then save it and view it in a Web browser. The next two chapters describe how you can take this fundamental knowledge and use it to author a personal home page. But for now, start with the essentials.

BEGIN WITH A TEMPLATE

All HTML documents have essential elements, so it is a good idea to create a template with these elements. You then can add text, graphics, or whatever to this template for your customized page.

(continued from previous page)

Line break

<hr>

Horizontal line or rule

HYPERTEXT LINKS

<a href="URL"> </a>

Enclosed text is link to another Web page

IMAGES

<img src="Image.format">

Adds an image to the document

TEMPLATE FOR TEST HTML PAGE

<html>

<head>

<title> </title>

</head>

<body>

</body>

</html>

If I were to use the template and fill in some basic information, my test document might look like this:

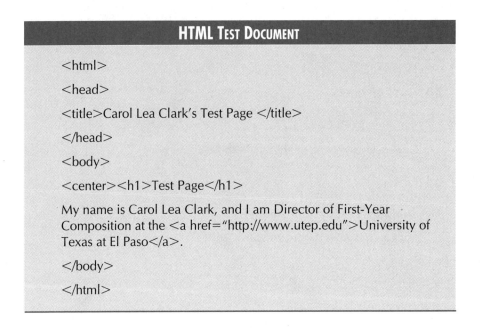

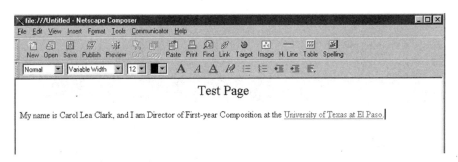

Text page viewed in Netscape.

Notice that even in this very basic document, I have made use of the World Wide Web technology by including a hypertext link to my university's home page. Of course, I probably would want to include more text about myself and my interests in a real home page, but this is a start. Once you know how to create an extremely basic home page, you can practice adding additional text and graphics. Chapters 9 and 10 elaborate on how to do so.

VIEW AN HTML DOCUMENT

You can view your test HTML document in a Web browser. In Netscape you use the pull-down *File* menu and select the *Open Page* option. In Internet Explorer, go to the pull-down *File* menu and select *Open*. In both cases, you will receive a dialog box where you can indicate the HTML document file name on your hard drive (or A drive if your file is on a floppy disk). Remember that an HTML document must have the file extension .htm or .html to be read by an Internet browser.

 # THINGS TO REMEMBER

1. HTML is white-space insensitive. When you are creating your HTML document, you may want to arrange it on the page much as you wish it to look on the browser screen. You must, however, use the paragraph tag <p> and line break tag <br> to indicate breaks in HTML because the browser otherwise will run everything together in one paragraph.

2. If you use a word processing program to create your HTML page, be sure to save the document as "text" if your word processor does not offer the option of saving it as an HTML document. Otherwise, your page may have embedded codes that will confuse a Web browser. Also, your file name must have the extension .htm or .html.

3. When using toggle codes such as the anchor code <a> . . . </a>, be certain your have included the second code with the slash (/) mark. A common mistake in HTML is omitting the closing code.

CHAPTER 9

Web Page Design

What are the essential traits of great Web sites? How can you bring your story to the world and actually get people to read it? Quality content and attractive graphics are certainly a good start. With a little careful planning, the fundamental traits of good Web page design discussed in this chapter can help you translate your ideas into Web pages. Most of the guidelines are simple common sense. With a good feel for the limitations and possibilities of Web publishing and a site plan in hand, you will have taken the first few steps toward creating a Web site you will be proud to submit to public scrutiny.

→ LIMITATIONS OF THE WEB

The World Wide Web, with its hypertext and hypermedia technology, offers vast but not limitless opportunities for creativity. You can use photographs, different type sizes and colors, background colors, and even video and sound. The Web, however, is primarily a vertical and list-oriented medium, making it difficult to do some tasks easily accomplished in desktop print publishing. Text in columns (like a newspaper), for example, is common in print but uncommon on the Web. Also, the low-resolution screens of today's personal computers affect a viewer's preferences and tolerances.

In your design, strive for a balance between visual sensation and text information. Shapes, colors, and contrast enliven a page. Dense text alone would be less interesting and more difficult to read. Highly graphical pages that are all color and flash without textual content are, however, equally unsatisfying to readers looking for information.

Consider Elements of Page Design

The elements of good page design are as important for Web pages as they are for printed documents. A well-designed document looks inviting and enhances the credibility of the information it contains. Some simple guidelines will help you design pleasing documents.

▼ Use space as a design element. Do not overcrowd your pages. Place materials so that important parts are emphasized by the space around them.

▼ Group information in chunks to make it easy to skim. Use headings and small text blocks. Most users dislike large sections of dense text and won't read them on the Web.

▼ Put important elements in the top left and lower right parts of the screen. English readers are trained to read from left to right, so their eyes naturally start at the upper left-hand corner of the screen. Their eyes, however, when skimming, don't flow line by line but move in a Z pattern, as illustrated in the diagram. If you put a heading or an important graphic at the upper left-hand corner, you will catch the reader's attention with that page element.

▼ All essential elements in a page, particularly a home page, should be in the 640 × 480 pixel screen size so that they appear when the page loads and readers do not have to scroll down the page (or even worse, across the page) to see important elements. Even if your readers have large monitors, the typical Netscape Navigator or Internet Explorer window still defaults to a win-

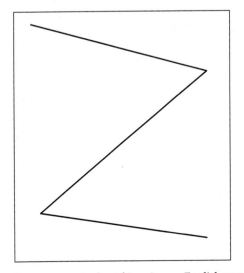

Eye movement when skimming an English page.

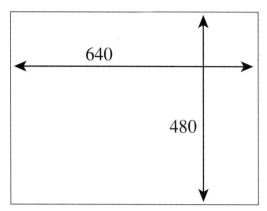

Ideal size for a home page (specified in pixels).

dow width designed for smaller monitors. Some design experts recommend an even smaller size for a home page: 535 pixels wide or more than about 320 pixels high.

▼ Be consistent. Provide a unified appearance for your pages so that they look like they belong together. This can be established with a template for your secondary pages, giving them all a similar look in terms of headings and other design elements.

▼ Arrange a clear and simple navigation between pages so that viewers can easily move from one page to to another.

▼ Use color, graphics, and symbols with restraint. By all means, take advantage of the hypermedia technology of the Web and use visual elements. Remember, however, that graphics take time to load and may make your readers impatient. It is advisable to limit your page to eighty kilobytes, including both text and graphics.

▼ Make your identity clear. Readers generally dislike pages without a specified author.

IDENTIFY YOUR PURPOSE

Whatever your chosen topic, you need to plan your pages. Define the purpose, policies, and individual objectives for your pages. Ask yourself these questions:

1.   Will your pages reflect your personality, interests, or abilities (such as a display of personal art or poetry or an online résumé)?

2. Will they educate your audience about a particular topic (such as security on the Internet or an organization at your university)?

3. Will they provide a service (bringing together reference materials about a topic such as Java programming or Queen Elizabeth I)?

Have a clear purpose. Remember, if you don't have a coherent objective for your pages, your readers won't see one either.

CONSIDER YOUR AUDIENCE

As you create your pages, always keep your audience in mind. Will they be people who are browsing casually or people who are seeking specific information? Think about what experience you want people to have when they visit your site. Do you

PURPOSE AND AUDIENCE ANALYSIS

You may find it beneficial to state your purpose and audience analysis in the form of a list of objectives. This list should define the specific goals that you want your Web site to accomplish. This will help you formulate a plan for conveying the topic to your audience.

Purpose of Web Site (state in one sentence)

Characteristics of Audience (state in one or two sentences)

Objective #1

Objective #2

Objective #3

Katherine Hughes, who authored the Dark Elegy page shown in the previous chapter and in the Web tour in Chapter 3, might have filled out the form this way:

EXAMPLE ➡

PURPOSE OF WEB SITE
To inform the public about a sculpture, Dark Elegy, which is a memorial to the passengers of Pan Am Flight 103, including 35 students from

(continued)

want them to get to know you, or would you like to point them toward research resources for a particular topic? Will your audience be actively or casually interested in what you present? If they are only casually interested in the material, they will have less patience about long text sections than will a highly committed audience. Realize that most people will skim your site, looking at graphics and headings and reading only sections that interest them. If you organize your material with meaningful headings, you make it easier for viewers to understand the content and follow the organization.

Consider which browser your audience will be using. You cannot assume your users will be reading your pages with the latest browser. They may be using an older version of Netscape or Explorer, or they may be using a text-only browser.

Do you anticipate that many of your viewers will be accessing via modem? If so, bandwidth is a consideration. Too many and too large graphics will slow downloading of your pages and may make users lose patience and abort the connection to your site.

(continued from previous page)
Syracuse [the author's university] who were killed in the 1988 airline bombing over Lockerbie, Scotland.

CHARACTERISTICS OF AUDIENCE
Individuals who have heard of the airplane bombing but who have not seen the sculpture. They will want to see details of the sculpture and learn some of its history, but they will be browsing, not looking for lengthy texts.

OBJECTIVE #1
Display the sculpture and explain why it was created.

OBJECTIVE #2
Place the sculpture in the context of what happened to the aircraft.

OBJECTIVE #3
Commemorate the loss of students' lives in the tragedy.

MAKE A VISUAL SITE PLAN

One of the best ways to take advantage of hypertext is to use a visual outline to plan your pages. Don't wait until you have all your content written before you begin planning the structure of your pages. Your goal is to have a unified and coherent set of Web pages that provides interesting and/or useful content presented in a consistent design framework. Your pages should look like they belong together and should make the information you present easily accessible to your user. It is best to have the two processes going on at the same time: writing the content and planning the content arrangement. This will make it easier to take advantage of the Web's hypertext capabilities.

To make a visual plan, decide which main information categories you want on your pages and put them in boxes; then organize the boxes into a logical structure that can be linked together. Here are a couple of basic layout structures:

a.   In a linear collection of pages, the viewer begins at the home page and moves from one page to the next. The only choices offered are to go forward, backward, and home.

b.   The hierarchical or branching-tree format is a more common design because it takes advantage of the Web's hypertext possibilities. On each page, visitors can choose "forks" or "branches" that lead them to other pages offering additional choices. From any page the viewer also can connect directly to the home page.

c.   Collections of pages usually are not symmetrical. You may, for example, have three pages under Topic 3 but none under Topic 2. You have no limit to the number of structure levels. It is best, however, to link pages only upward and downward in a hierarchical tree. If you connect sideways as well, you can confuse your reader, who will have trouble maintaining a sense of location in the pages.

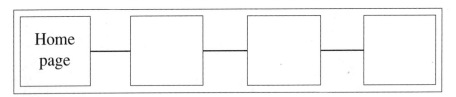

a. Linear "all in line" format.

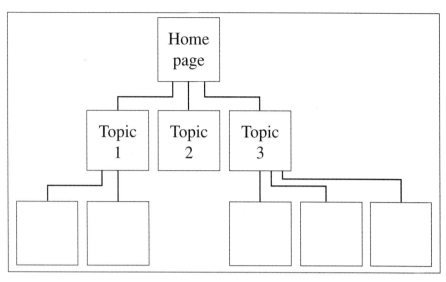

b. Hierarchical or branching-tree format.

 ## Example of a Site Plan

Katherine Hughes's Dark Elegy site (you saw her home page in Chapter 8) follows the branching outline; see p. 138.

Hughes's site is of medium size, with sixteen pages she has created and linked to related sites at other locations. The site is well organized, covering the topic and offering interesting photographs and other graphics. It is a polished, well-thought-out presentation.

 ## Plan Your Home Page

Your home page is the first page a viewer sees when connecting to your pages. It is an introductory map to your site and should be concise. It must introduce your subject, giving enough information in text and/or graphics so that your viewers can tell whether they want to know more. Graphics should be kept relatively small (in terms of file size), and page size should be kept to 640 × 480 pixels if possible. Visitors may be irritated if they have to spend several minutes waiting

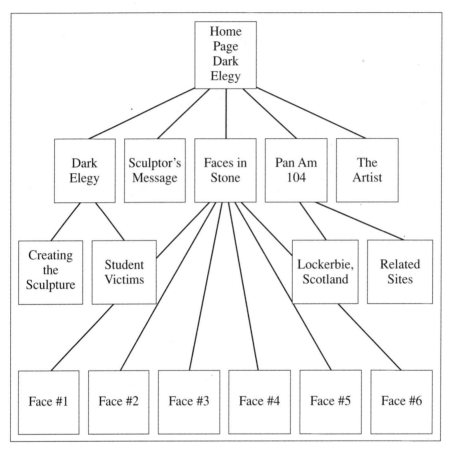

Outline of the Dark Elegy site.

for a home page graphic to load. Ideally, your home page should be organized so that viewers with text-only browsers can navigate it, which means you need to give text alternatives for any graphics or graphical links, including text alternatives to any navigation buttons. Include contact information, usually in the form of an e-mail address at the bottom of the page, so that readers can reach you with comments or questions.

Just because the home page is the first page your viewers see does not mean it is the first page you should perfect. It is probably best to produce a draft home page with a list of links to your other pages, but you may want to spend time first on your secondary pages before you produce a polished version of your home page. As you develop and change them, they will affect your home page content.

CREATE A TEMPLATE FOR SECONDARY PAGES

Your Web pages should be designed with a consistent look and feel. Examine collections of Web pages on the Net, choose ones you like, and notice how a particular individual's secondary pages (those that aren't the home page) relate to each other. They may have a common header or graphic at the top of the page, and backgrounds will be coordinated. The body of each page will be organized in a similar fashion, with text and graphics placed consistently, though they will vary in content.

To create your own template for a Web page, use a basic template like the one reproduced in the previous chapter or the one next, which includes a few more elements, such as an address. Take one of the two or three screen-length chunks you have composed for one of your secondary pages and insert it in the template. Play with it, creating headings, using type styles and graphics, and so on, until you have a format you like.

SAMPLE TEMPLATE

```
<html>
<head>
<title>Name or Title of the Page</title>
</head>
<body>
<h2>Title of the Page</h2>
Place your text here.
<p>
<a href="http:URLofyourhomepage">Home</a>
<p>
<Address>
Created by Your Name <br>
<a href=mailto:yourlogin@yourschool.edu>
yourlogin@yourschool.edu</a>
</Address>
</body>
</html>
```

As you design your template, remember to include navigational links to direct your site's flow from one page to another. Try to put yourself in the place of the user's who will be reading your site. Do the links connect to each other in a logical fashion? Are the links placed to optimize the speed for uses to find key information?

 # PLAN YOUR GRAPHICS

One of the most appealing features of the World Wide Web is its capability to display colorful images. Well-chosen graphics can make a Web page come alive for readers, entertaining while enhancing their understanding of the content. Graphics, however, must be relevant to the page content, or they will distract or mislead readers. Be aware that each image you use will delay downloading of the page, so use restraint when deciding on numbers of images. Also, try to keep the size of each graphic to under twenty kilobytes. If you want to use larger images, try putting a thumbnail version of the image on your page and using it as a link to a page with a larger version of the image.

Generally, graphics used on the Web are saved in one of two formats: GIF (Graphics Interchange Format) and JPEG (Joint Photographic Experts Group—the developers). The difference between the two is the technique used to store the image. The JPEG format offers more colors, but its compression technique can blur a picture slightly. GIF images don't have as many colors but will not degrade in clarity. Consult Chapter 8 and Chapter 10 for more information about graphics.

Note: A frequent error made with graphics is using graphics that are too wide to appear in the screen of common browsers. This makes the graphic spill off the side of the pages and forces readers to scroll to the right to see the rest of your graphic. Test your graphic to be sure it is not too wide (try using a width limit of 472 pixels if your graphic is to appear full screen).

 # NAVIGATIONAL TOOLS

If a page's author does not provide adequate navigational tools, visitors can become lost in cyberspace. Visitors should be able to return to your home page from any page within your site.

Graphical navigational tools add a polished look to your pages, but be careful that your audience knows what the graphical icons mean. "Home" is a common term and one your audience generally will understand to mean your cover or home page. Here is an example of an icon used for home on Web pages. Numerous others are available in collections of icons and graphics (see the next chapter for a list of such collections).

If you decide to use several graphical navigation buttons, it is best to use text labels also; this helps any visitor who may not understand your buttons and also provides a navigation mechanism for visitors who are connecting via a text-only browser.

A portion of Katherine Hughes's home page shown here displays redundant navigational tools. She created thumbnail images as links to secondary pages and also gives text alternates just below her images.

An example of redundant graphic and text navigational tools.

 ## QUALITY CONTROL

Examine your pages carefully. Check your spelling. Test the links to see that they all work. View your document in more than one browser; you can't assume that what looks great in Netscape will look as good in all browsers. Even if you don't update your pages regularly, check the links periodically because Web addresses change.

 ## WHAT'S IN A GREAT WEB SITE?

Several important rules separate the good pages from the great ones. A great Web site will

▼ *Provide valuable, timely information to the user*. This means your Web site should be updated regularly.

▼ *Provide credible, original content in as many forms as possible.* Original content is one of the most important traits of a great Web site. Sites that constantly provide the most complete and up-to-date information will stand out in the crowd.

▼ *Be easy to read.* Pages that use backgrounds that are almost the same shade as the text are difficult to read and will turn readers away. Remember to use white space and to stick to colors that are not hard on the eyes.

▼ *Be well organized.* Divide your text logically into chunks of closely related information. Provide multiple forms of intuitive interpage navigation (clickable arrows, graphic icons, and hypertext links). Balance the number of levels in your hierarchical design with page length to minimize scrolling and display time.

▼ *Be innovative.* Provide users with information or services they can't find anywhere else. Update your site regularly, and offer activities that will keep users coming back for more.

ONLINE RESOURCES

A number of online Web page design guides exist, including the following. You can also use the search engines, giving keywords such as *authoring* and *World Wide Web and style* to find others.

WWW Style Manual (at yale)

http://info.med.yale.edu/caim/manual/contents.html

HTML Style Guide

http://www.w3.org/hypertext/WWW/Provider/Style/Introduction

Sun Guide to Web Style

http://www.sun.com/styleguide

The Sevloid Guide to Web Design

http://www.sev.com.au/webzone/design.htm

You also can review Web pages for examples at several sites, as noted earlier. Personal Pages Worldwide: College and University Collections, http://www.utexas.edu/world/personal, gives links to collections of personal pages at colleges and universities worldwide. You can examine other student pages by connecting to university home pages and looking for the link *Student Pages*. Yahoo's List of Personal Home Pages, **http://www.yahoo.com/Society and Culture/People/Personal Home Pages,** links to more than 50,000 home pages in the United States. You can suggest adding your home page to the list by clicking on *Suggest a Site* and following the directions.

CHAPTER 10

Web Page Authoring Techniques

After reading the preceding chapters, you should have a basic working knowledge of HTML and an awareness of Web page design. Now's the time to learn some of the intermediate Web page authoring techniques that can help you implement your plans for great Web pages.

BACKGROUND COLORS

Adding a background color or texture to your pages can greatly enhance visual appeal. To add a background color or texture, you need to alter the <body> tag, located near the beginning of your Web page. Background colors are made up of a six-digit, hexadecimal (digits ranging from 0 to f; i.e., 123 . . . 89abcdef) code, which controls the appearance of the background in the browser window. The attribute for a white background, for example, would read <body bgcolor="#ffffff">, with the code ffffff for white. The six-digit code represents a red-green-blue set of numeric values, two characters for each value.

Also, HTML recognizes sixteen widely used color names. They are listed here:

HTML RECOGNIZED COLOR NAMES
Black = "#000000"
Green = "#008000"
Silver = "#c0c0c0"
Lime = "#00ff00"
Gray = "#808080"
Olive = "#808000"
White = "#ffffff"
Yellow = "#ffff00"
Maroon = "#800000"
Navy = "#000080"
Red = "#ff0000"
Blue = "#0000ff"
Purple = "#800080"
Teal = "#008080"
Fuchsia = "#ff00ff"
Aqua = "#00ffff"

For the colors given, you don't need to give the hexadecimal numbers. If you want a red background, for example, you simply can say <body bgcolor=red>.

Guides to background colors can be found at a number of sites on the Web. A quick way to find the exact color you are looking for is to connect to one of these sites, choose the color you like, and record the hexadecimal number. If you like the turquoise color you see on one of these pages, for example, you would record the number 3333ff. Then you could use it as a background color with this tag:

<body bgcolor="3333ff">

Among the sites that offer *nondithering* hexadecimal colors are Lynda Weinman's Non-Dithering Colors in Browsers, **http://www.lynda.com/hex.html**, and Infinet Colors, http://www.infi.net/wwwimages/colorindex.html. A *dithering* color is one some browsers create by combining color dots in a pattern to make up the desired color. Sometimes this pattern effect is distracting. Choose a color from one of these pages or others that provide nondithering colors, and your colors should be consistent. If you want to use colors you find elsewhere and to be certain they will not dither, a solution is to create a small block of the color in a graphics program and treat it as a background pattern (described next), not a color.

 # BACKGROUND IMAGES

Background images may be photographs, graphics, or colored textures. Like other images on the Web, they are generally in either GIF or JPEG file format. When a browser displays a background image, it repeats the image, starting in the upper left-hand corner of the browser window and working across and down until the entire background of the page is covered with the image. If the image is large, it may fill the entire background of the page. If the image is a small one, it is repeated many, many times. This can lead to a tiling effect as the image repeats over and over again. An image can be carefully drawn so that the edges of the image flow seamlessly into the next image as the images are tiled across the screen. If you use a little imagination, your background images can improve the look of almost any page.

The tag for a background image is very similar to the tag for a background color. However, rather than choosing a color code, you first need to specify the file name of the image you wish to use as the background image. Second, the tag BGCOLOR should be changed to the tag BACKGROUND. Therefore, if you wanted to use a file named "texture.gif" as the background image for your page, you would use the tag <body background="texture.gif">.

You can create a background texture or graphic yourself in a graphics program or copy the background from another Web site. Netscape, for example, offers a selection of backgrounds at http://home.netscape.com/assist/net_sites/bg/backgrounds.html. Use the same technique to obtain these that you would use for copying images. Position your cursor over the image pattern presented in a rectangle. If you are using a Windows version of Netscape, press the right mouse button, or if you are using a Macintosh version, hold down the mouse button for about a second. In either case, a dialog box will appear that allows you to save the image to your disk. Then simply give the file name of the GIF or JPEG file in your <body> attribute, and the pattern will fill the background of your page. Many other background archives exist on the Web. Consult the box on pp. 148–149 for additional sites.

If you find a background on an existing Web page you would like to copy, you can use the same procedure as discussed for copying images but slightly modified.

You can copy only images, not whole backgrounds, from Web pages, so you must direct your Web browser to access the image file used as the background and then copy that image file. You do this by looking at the source code for the document and recording the name of the background file in the body background tag <body background="name.gif">. (Both Netscape Navigator and Internet Explorer offer an selection from the View menu which allows you to see HTML source code.) Then call up the image file by amending the URL address of the page. For example, if the name of the background is "redtie.gif" and the URL of the page is **http://www. university.edu/~student/home.html**, then you can call up the .gif file by using this code:

http://www.university.edu/~student/redtie.gif

When you connect to this file, your browser will display it just like any other image file, which you then can copy. Remember, image backgrounds that are photographs, logos, or unique combinations of symbols are considered copyrighted. You need to obtain permission to use them, just as you would with any other image.

Caution: When selecting colors, textures, or images, check to make sure the page remains readable. A busy background can make it difficult to read the page.

ARCHIVES OF BACKGROUND COLORS, TEXTURES, AND IMAGES

Locate other archives by going to your favorite search engine and consulting subject headings Web page design. Or try searching for key words such as "backgrounds" or "colors."

Ace of Space

http://www.aceofspace.com

The Backgrounds Archive

http://www.pixelfoundry.com/bgs.html

Freeimages.com

http://www.freeimages.com

Free Webpage Designs

http://www.geocities.com/WallStreet/1679/backgrounds.html

Imagine

http://imagine.metanet.com

Infinet Colors

http://www.infi.net/wwwimages/colorindex.html

(continued)

Try to view your page with the background color or texture in more than one browser and on more than one monitor. What looks great in Netscape with a high-quality monitor may be difficult to read in another browser or with a sixteen-color display. Also, textured backgrounds displayed with some monitors or nonstandard browsers may obscure your text. If you understate your background colors or textures, you are less likely to create a page that is hard to read in a different browser or on a reduced-color monitor.

 ## TEXT FONT, COLOR, AND SIZE

HTML now offers you the ability to change typeface font, size, and color. Caution is needed for this, however. Font face and color depends to a large degree on the computer and browser used to view your page. You may specify an interesting font and because some viewers do not have that font loaded on their computer, they will instead see the default font, which is Times Roman. Color combinations

(continued from previous page)

Lynda Weinman's Non-Dithering Colors in Browsers

http://www.lynda.com/hex.html

Moby's Icon Archive

http://www.dsv.su.se/~matti-hu/archive.html

Netscape's Backgrounds

http://home.netscape.com/assist/net_sites/bg/backgrounds.html

Pardon My Icons

http://www.zeldman.com

Texture Land

http://www.meat.com/textures

WebSoc Graphics Library

http://www.gla.ac.uk/Clubs/WebSoc/graphics

of font and background will appear differently on different computers and browsers, so what looks wonderful on your monitor may be possibly unreadable on someone else's. Again, it is important to view your page on more than one computer and, preferably, with more than one browser to reduce the chances of font and color glitches.

To change any of the font attributes at any time within your page, simply use the <font> tag. The text that follows will remain changed until you close with the </font> tag. Some commonly used typeface fonts are Times New Roman, Arial, MS Sans Serif, Garamond, Verdana, Impact, Arial Black, and Arial Narrow. If you wanted to try Arial Narrow, for example, you would use the tag <font face="Arial Narrow">.

If you want to modify your text color, you can use the same color codes used for backgrounds and change your <font> tag. White text, for example, would have the code <font color="ffffff">. To enlarge the size of your type slightly, use the tag <font size="+1">, use +2 for larger, and so on. To turn off the type size or color you have specified, use the tag </font>.

You can string together tags for color, typeface font, and size. For example, your tag could read <font face="Arial Narrow" color="#ffffff" size="+3">.

TEXT GRAPHICS

An easy and effective way to add visual interest to your Web page is to create a text graphic for use as a title (not in the title bar) or heading. You can use any of a number of draw, paint, or image-manipulation programs to do this. Or you can copy an image from a clip-art program and add text. Or you can find creative fonts on the Web. The title graphic ("Web Page Design") given here was composed in ClarisWorks Paint for the Macintosh and cropped in Graphic Converter, a shareware editor for the Macintosh. It is simply thirty-six-point white text over a color background.

Web Page Design

Alternatively, you could use Adobe Photoshop, Graphic Workshop, Paint Shop Pro, or any number of other graphics tools to create your text graphic. The following graphic is a montage of images united in one graphic.

The program you use to create your text graphic must be able to save your text graphic as a GIF or JPEG image, already noted as the two image formats most

commonly supported by various Web browsers. If you are using a computer in your college or university's lab, you likely will have graphics programs available to you. If you are using your home computer, you also may wish to keep a toolbox of common graphics programs, many of which are available as shareware or freeware, that can assist you with basic formatting procedures, such as cropping and manipulating the image or adjusting the number and intensity of the colors used in the image. You can find these programs on the Web by looking in one of the search engines under *software*.

Once you have completed your title graphic, you can include it in your HTML document with an image source tag like the following: <img src="title.gif">. If this is to be a title graphic, it should be placed on the page wherever the page title best fits. A simple page might include the tag just after the <body> tag, placing the title graphic at the very top of the user's browser window. The title does not need to be simple text. You can create extremely complicated and striking images for title graphics. Still, even a basic graphic looks more polished than a <font size ="+3"> tag would create in HTML.

 ## SCANNING IMAGES

Photos and graphics add impressive visual interest to Web pages. To include existing nonelectronic images, such as drawings or photographs, on your Web page, you will need to scan the images. Scanning creates a digital copy of an image, which then can be edited by a graphics editor on your computer and used as an image file by a Web browser. Many colleges and universities have scanners available to students. Check with the computer lab administrator at your university to find out how you can access scanning facilities.

Just as you can use many programs to edit graphics, many programs also allow you to scan images. These programs are sometimes included with the scanner as part of a package deal. Common programs include DeskScan, ImageMaker, and Adobe Photoshop. Using one of these programs should be fairly self-explanatory, though the lab staff likely will be willing to demonstrate the software for you, and manuals should be available.

The basic procedure for scanning a picture begins with you placing your photo or image facedown on the scanner glass and instructing the scanning program to preview the image. It will scan the image and present the preview in a window for you to evaluate. Use the tools offered in the preview window to adjust the preview until it is suitable to scan. You probably won't want to scan the image at a resolution greater than 72 dpi (dots per inch), as the extra resolution only will add to the file size of your image. Most scanning programs will give you several options for saving the image. Save the image in a format that a graphics editor can interpret (preferably in GIF or JPEG format).

Once you have scanned the image, you still may need to edit it before it is ready for the Web. You will need to resize the graphic, determining the height and width the image will occupy when it appears on a Web page; to adjust the brightness, contrast, and sharpness of the image; and to manipulate the file size by altering the number of colors used. Most scanning software will allow you to perform some if not all of these functions before you save the file; however, if the program does not allow you to do this, you may need to use a graphics editor to make the appropriate modifications.

When you alter the size of a graphic, make sure to double-check the size using a Web browser. Use the procedure described in Chapter 8 for viewing a test page in a browser, except your graphic file will have the extension **.gif** or **.jpg** (see the following section on image formats).

You also can alter the size of your image as it will appear on your Web page by altering the IMG SRC tag. You can specify the size of the image either in pixels or a percentage of the width of the Web page. For example, if you wanted your image to be one hundred pixels in width, you would use the image source tag <img src="photo1.gif" width=100>. If you wanted to specify it in a percentage, you would use <img src="photo1.gif" width=25%> or whatever percentage you desired. The height would be adjusted in proportion to the width.

Use a reduced number of colors for your images unless detail is critical. Fifty colors generally will reproduce adequately on eight-bit (256-color) screens and will take much less time to download. Your graphics editor should be able to reduce the number of colors in the color palette your image uses.

 # IMAGE FORMATS

Only a few image formats are supported by most Web browsers. As noted earlier, the primary formats are the GIF family of encoding schemes and the JPEG compression scheme. GIF and JPEG image formats are each best suited to particular jobs. A GIF image is a good choice for buttons, simple title graphics, icons, and many images. GIF images can contain a transparent color, which allows them to merge with backgrounds and blend into a page more completely. The GIF format can create very precise images. However, this comes with a price. GIFs have a limit of 256 colors and do not compress as compactly as JPEGs. The color limit means that while the GIF format is great for many images, it is not the best choice for images with many different colors, such as a photograph of a busy street.

The JPEG format is great for photographs. The compression scheme used in JPEG processing does lose some data, but it allows you to compress a complicated image to a very compact size. JPEG images can contain millions of colors and are best suited to displaying photographs, gradient images (where colors fade from one to the next like a rainbow), and complex designs. Displaying JPEG files processing often takes longer than GIF files, which is also an important factor to consider when deciding which format to use.

Note: A GIF graphics file will always have the extension .gif after the file name. A JPEG file will have a .jpeg extension, if it is generated on a Macintosh. If created on any other computer, a JPEG file will have a .jpg extension.

GIF

The Graphics Interchange Format, or GIF, is a no-loss method of compression created by CompuServe. So what does "no loss" mean? No-loss compression uses a mathematical algorithm that reduces the size of the graphic file without losing any of the information contained within that file. If the algorithm comes across several identical parts of the image data, it substitutes a single character for those sections of the file, thus reducing the file's size. As it makes these substitutions, the algorithm builds a "hash" table that remembers all of the substituted items so that a GIF decoder, such as your Web browser, can decode the compressed image. For example, an image file might contain the sequence of digits 112233, 112233, 112233. The algorithm substitutes the number 1 for the string 112233 everywhere it encounters that string. Using this system, the sequence 112233, 112233, 112233 is reduced to 1, 1, 1. As the algorithm makes the substitution, it adds a line to the hash table that says something like 112233=1. That way, when the image is read by your Web browser, the browser knows to substitute 112233 everywhere it reads a 1 in the graphic data.

GIF images are governed by a couple rules. First, because a GIF is limited to a color palette of 256 colors, the GIF format is ideal for some graphics but may not be the best choice for photograph-quality images. Second, although GIF is a compact image format, it is not always the most compact. Due to the method of compression used in a GIF image, images with a large amount of repetition, such as images made up primarily of a single flat color, will compress very well, while a complex image with many colors and less repetition, such as a photograph of a crowded room, will not compress as well.

JPEG

The JPEG compression scheme derives its name from the committee originally responsible for its development, the Joint Photographic Experts Group. JPEG uses a "lossy" compression algorithm. This means that unlike GIF images, JPEG images do not contain all of the data from the original picture. Instead of compressing the existing data, the JPEG algorithm divides the image into a series of squares. Next, it uses a mathematical technique called Discrete Cosine Transformation to transform each square into a set of mathematically defined curves. As the image is compressed, the algorithm removes the less significant curves from the image. This does two things. First, with these pieces of data removed, the amount of data is considerably reduced. The second effect however is the loss of some of the fine detail in the image. A radically compressed JPEG image can appear as just a rough assortment of blocks with little or no resemblance to the original image. Most graphic editors that support JPEG compression will give you the ability to choose the level of compression you wish to use. As you choose higher compression rates, the quality of the final image will deteriorate, so take care when balancing file size against image quality.

 # TRANSPARENT IMAGES

Transparent images are useful when you are trying to blend an image into its background or trying to use an image that is an unusual shape. A transparent image is an image saved in GIF format with one of the colors set as "see through." Many new Web authors face the problem of trying to draw a round graphic and make it appear round on their Web page. Graphics editors only allow you to save rectangular images. You can draw a circle, but the image you save is a rectangle containing the circle. So how do you get rid of all of the extra area surrounding the circle? The simplest way is to make the extraneous part of the image transparent.

To make part of an image transparent, you will need to save it as a GIF, so remember to limit the image to 256 colors or less. Some, though not all, graphics editors will have a transparency option. This allows you to select a color out of the GIF color palette to match the background color of the image and set the color as transparent. Once you have done this, any color displayed behind the image, such as the background color in the Web browser, will show through the transparent parts of the image. If your favorite graphics editor does not support the transparency effect, a number of shareware programs create transparent colors (an example of this is Transparency for the Macintosh). Be careful when assigning the transparent color. If you are working with a drawing of a forest and you make the color green transparent, all of your trees will disappear.

CONTROLLING IMAGE DOWNLOAD TIME

Simple Web graphics can be enhanced to improve performance and to add interesting visual effects. A common Web problem is the amount of time required to download even a medium-sized image. Improperly formatted images contribute to the long delays often caused by low-speed modem links to the Web. Several techniques have been developed to alleviate this problem. Image file sizes should be kept small, under twenty kilobytes if possible. To achieve this size image file, the total number of colors also should be kept relatively small, preferably under 150 colors per image. Never use a resolution greater than 72 dpi for Web graphics. Most computer screens do not display more than 72 dpi, and therefore a higher resolution would be a waste. The GIF and JPEG image formats are among the most compact and flexible formats available (hence their extensive use on the Web), and they allow Web designers and graphic artists to control all of these variables.

A common way to improve download time is to use thumbnail images. A thumbnail is a scaled-down copy of the original image linked to the original image. A thumbnail gives users an opportunity to view an image without downloading a large file. If users decide to view the full-size version of a thumbnail image, all they have to do is click on the thumbnail, and the browser will download and display the full-size image.

Creating a thumbnail image is simple. First, use a graphics editor such as one of those discussed earlier to create a scaled-down copy of your image. Then, when creating your page, connect the image tag to the scaled-down copy, This is

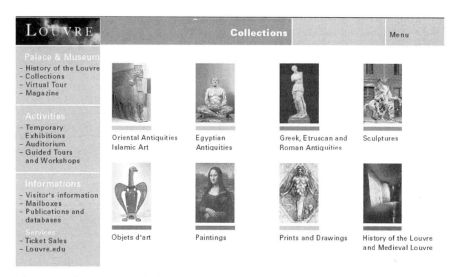

The Louvre home page includes thumbnail images that are hot links to full-screen versions of the images.

the thumbnail image. Second, enclose the image tag in a link to the full-size version so that when a user clicks on your thumbnail image, the full-scale version will be downloaded. For example, if the thumbnail image is named "tnail-gif" and the full-size image is named "fsize.gif," you would use the following tag in your HTML file: <a href="fsize.gif"><img src="tnail.gif"></a>.

SHAPING YOUR DESIGN: THE TABLE TAG

The table tag is a powerful and popular one because of its ability to create blocks on a Web page for organizing information. Originally created to allow even spacing for data tables, tables can contain any type of information. They can enclose text, images, links, or a combination of these. The following is a navigational text and graphic table from the Dark Elegy home page discussed in Chapter 9:

CREATING A TABLE

To create a table, begin with the <table> and </table> tags, which must come before and after the entire table. Each horizontal row of information, whether data, text, or images, is defined independently by the table row tags <tr> and </tr>. Within a row, the table entries are defined by the table data tags <td> and </td>. Table data tags must only appear within a pair of table row tags. The area within the table data tags is referred to as a *cell*. All rows do not have to have the same number of cells. The table data tags create cells from left to right across a row, and if one row has fewer cells than another, the short row will be padded with blank cells to make up the difference. Any of the HTML tags normally present in the body of an HTML document can be used within a pair of table data tags.

The code for a very basic table, with explanations in the parentheses, might look like this:

<table border=numberofpixels> (beginning of table, border size specified in pixels)

<caption></caption> (caption for table)

<tr> (beginning of first row)

<td></td> (first table entry in row 1)

<td></td> (second table entry in row 1)

</tr> (end of first row)

<tr> (beginning of second row)

<td></td> (first table entry in row 2)

<td></td> (second table entry in row 2)

</tr> (end of second row)

<tr> (beginning of row 3)

<td> </td> (first table entry in row 3)

<td> </td> (last table entry in row 3)

</tr> (end of third row)

</table>

Using the table attributes (between tags) discussed in the following box, you can customize your own tables on your Web pages.

MODIFYING ATTRIBUTES FOR HTML TABLES

TABLE BORDER

The *border* attribute controls whether or not borders are drawn around the table cells and what width the border should be. For example, <table border=4> would create a table with a border four pixels wide. By default the cells in a table are separated by one pixel, whether or not the border attribute is in use; however this can be removed by setting a value of zero within the table border tag.

ALIGN

The *align* modifier controls placement of all data within a cell. If the ALIGN attribute appears with a table row or table data tag, it controls whether the data within the tags is aligned to the left, right, or center (i.e., align=center). If the ALIGN attribute appears within the caption tags, <caption></caption>, it controls whether the caption appears above or below the table. The attribute within a caption would read either align=top or align=bottom.

CELLPADDING

Cell padding controls the amount of space between the border of a cell and the content of the cell. Using the cell padding attribute can give a wide-open look to a table, often making the table a bit easier to read. For example, to create a table with four pixels of space around the data in the cell, you would use the tag <table cellpadding=4>

(continued)

(continued from previous page)

CELLSPACING

Cell spacing is the amount of space inserted between the cells in a table. For example, if you want to insert a space four pixels wide between the cells in a table, you would use the tag <table cellspacing=4>.

COLSPAN

The COLSPAN attribute allows you to create a data cell that spans more than one column in the table. The attribute is used with the table data tags. For example, in order to create a cell that spans two columns within a table, you would use <td colspan=2>.

ROWSPAN

The ROWSPAN attribute works exactly like the COLSPAN attribute, but changes the number of vertical rows a cell occupies.

VALIGN

The VALIGN modifier is similar to the align modifier in that it controls the placement of data within a cell. The VALIGN modifier appears within a <tr> or <td> tag and controls the vertical alignment of data within a particular row or cell. Data can be aligned to the top, middle, bottom, or baseline of the cell.

WIDTH

The *width* attribute controls the width of a table or cell, either as a percentage of the width of the browser screen or as an absolute width in pixels. For example, the tag <table width=50%> would create a table that occupies 50 percent of the screen width. Alternatively, when used with the table data tag, <td width=50%> would create a cell that occupies exactly half the width of the table.

A table that contains images, such as the table from the Dark Elegy page reproduced on p. 156, would have <img src> tags placed in the table as data. The HTML code for the Dark Elegy image table looks like this:

SOURCE CODE FOR THE DARK ELEGY IMAGE TABLE

```
<table width=462 cellpadding=0 border=0>

<tr>
```

(continued)

(continued from previous page)

```
    <td width=66><a href="http:DARKELEGY1.html"><img
border=0 src="a.gif"></a></td>

    <td width=98><a href="http:MESSAGE.html"><img border=0
src="b.gif"></a></td>

    <td width=78><a href="http:FACES.html"><img border=0
src="c.gif">/a>/td>

    <td width=70><a href="http:PAN_AM.html"><img border=0
src="d.gif"></a></td>

    <td width=84><a href="http:ARTIST.html"><img border=0
src="e.gif"></a></td>

    <td width=66><a href="http:deindex.html"><img border=0
src="f.gif"></a></td>

    </tr>

    </table>
```

The first line of code for the Dark Elegy table indicates the table width in pixels and specifies no table border. Each cell (or box) in the border has a slightly different size, which is specified by the <td width=size> code. This is followed by the URL of the link, then the image source for the image in each cell. Note that the text in the table is part of the images and is not separate HTML data. The author has edited the text and images together in a graphics program and saved the combination as GIF images such as this one:

Tables require some time and effort, but the outcome is very effective visually. You may find it helpful to locate a table on the Internet, such as the Dark Elegy one, that you would like to adapt for your own graphics. Examine the image source code, and compare it to the table as it appears in your browser. (Both Netscape Navigator and Internet Explorer offer a selection from the *View* menu which allows you to see HTML source code.) You can learn from what others have created.

CREATING A SIMPLE PERSONAL PAGE

You can create your personal Web site with an infinite variety of content. The following Web page is simple but attractive. If you follow the directions given here, you can author a similar one for yourself.

Jessica D. Stephenson

"When one door closes, another opens. But we often look so regretfully upon the closed door that we don't see the one that has been opened for us "
Alexander Graham Bell

The page has the student's name; a photo, background graphic, and quote; links to secondary pages; and a link to an e-mail address. Let's look at how those appear on the HTML page and then discuss each element separately. Here all the HTML codes are highlighted in bold so you can see them more easily, though you won't want to do that with your own HTML page.

CODES FOR JESSICA D. STEPHENSON'S PAGE

```
<html>
<head>
<title>Jessica's Web Page</title>
</head>
<body text="#006600" background="ivyback.jpg">
```

(continued)

(continued from previous page)

```
<center> <b><font size="+3">Jessica D. Stephenson</font>
</b><p><img src="photo.jpg">
```

"When one door closes, another opens. But we often look so regretfully
`<br>` upon the closed door that we don't see the one that has been opened
for us." `<br>`Alexander Graham Bell`<br>`

```
<p><a href="essaylin.htm"><img SRC="inyessay.jpg"></a>
<a href="mailto:jesstep@xuniversity.edu"><img src="ivye-mail.
jpg"></a>
<a href="resume.htm"><img src="ivyresume.jpg"></a>
<a href="photos.htm"><img src="ivymystery.jpg"></a>
</center>
</body>
</html>
```

As we analyze this HTML page, remember that HTML is white-space insensitive, which means it doesn't matter if you add spaces in your text on the HTML page. If you add a line break but don't indicate the `<BR>` tag, for example, the browser will not display your page with that line break. Again, HTML tags are also case insensitive, which means that `<html>` and `<HTML>` are the same tag. Now, let's look at each element of the HTML page separately:

```
<html>
<head>
<title>Jessica's Web Page</title>
</head>
```

Begin your page with the `<html>` tag. Next comes the `<head>` tag for header, then the title tag just before the title of your page. This title won't appear on your Web page itself. Some Web browser versions display the title at the top of the browser screen, and it is also used by automated search engines to classify your page.

<body text="#006600" background="ivyback.jpg">

Modifies the <body> tag to include specification of green text that matches the green ivy in the background image. Also specifies a background image. Here the name of the image file is **ivyback.jpg** If you prefer to use a solid background color, the tag would read <body bdcolor="000000">, assuming you were using a solid black background.

<font size="+3">Jessica D. Stephenson</font>

The <center> toggle tag tells the browser to center all elements until it sees the </center> tag. The +3 size is appropriate for a headline. After the text "Jessica D. Stephenson," comes the </font> which turns off the font color and size. The <br> stands for line break.

<p><img src="photo.jpg">

The <p> tag stands for paragraph and inserts a line of blank space. The <img src> tag is used to locate an image in the page. In this case, the name of the image is photo.jpg.

<p>

Adds a line of space.

"When one door closes, another opens. But we often look so regretfully <br> upon the closed door that we don't see the one that has been opened for us."
Alexander Graham Bell
<p>

This text is centered on the page because of the <center> command earlier. The <br> at the end of each line indicates a line break. If you didn't insert the <br> command, the text would word wrap. The <p> adds a blank line.

<a href="essaylin.htm"><img SRC="inyessay.jpg"></a>

<a href="mailto:jesstep@xuniversity.edu"><img src="ivye-mail.jpg"></a>

<a href="resume.htm"><img src="ivyresume.jpg"></a>

<a href="photos.htm"><img src="ivymystery.jpg"></a>

These are the hot links to additional pages. The <href> command indicates hypertext reference which means a link. What falls between the <a href> and the <a> command is a hot link. In this case the hot links are small images that work as buttons. The anchors could also be text.

Turns off the center command.

> **</body>**

Ends the body of the html page.

> **</html>**

Ends the html page.

 ## USING NETSCAPE'S BUILT-IN EDITOR TO CREATE A WEB PAGE

As noted, a number of HTML editors are available for constructing a Web page without learning the HTML tag codes. Netscape Navigator has one called Composer included in its browser program. The following demonstration will describe all the steps necessary to author the same student home page in Netscape that was created earlier with HTML tags.

Go to the Netscape Navigator *File* menu and select *New* and then *Blank Page*.

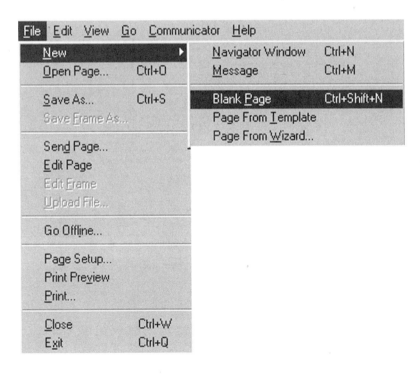

You will see the Composer screen with a blank space where you can create your Web page. Here the student's heading is already entered.

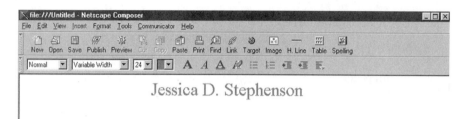

This text was created by selecting the typeface, size, and type color from the pull-down menus on the Composer screen:

The first menu on the left allows you to select heading size if you want. Or, you can just choose a type size in the third menu from the left. Choose a typeface in the second menu from the left. Select type color by clicking on the fourth menu and choosing a color. If you like, you can select bold, italics, underlined type by clicking on one of the *A*'s.

Center your text by clicking the alignment button and selecting centered text. The alignment button looks like this:

Next, you can select a background image by going to the *Format* menu and selecting *Page Colors* and *Properties*. You will see this dialog box, where you can input the name of your image file or search for it by clicking on *Choose File*. When you have selected your background image, click on *OK*.

If you want to include a photograph, position your cursor where you want the photo to go, and click on the *Image* icon on the Composer screen. You will see an *Image Properties* dialog box similar to the following one. Click on *Choose File* to select an image from your hard drive or disk. Once you have selected one (and edited it, if you choose, using *Edit Image* and other options shown), click on *OK*, and it will appear in your Composer screen window.

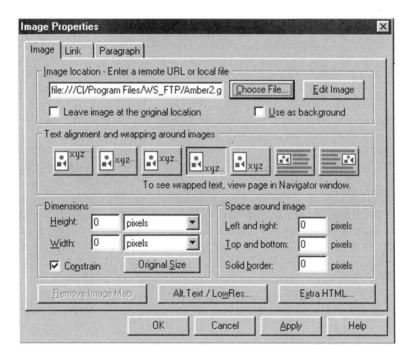

To create a hypertext link, highlight the text you want to be the hot link, and then click on the *Link* icon. You will see the following dialog box. Type in the address of the Web page you want to link to, and then click on *OK*. Jessicas's Web page uses small images as buttons rather than having text as hot links. If you want the same effect, insert the images for your buttons using the method described above and then make them hot links.

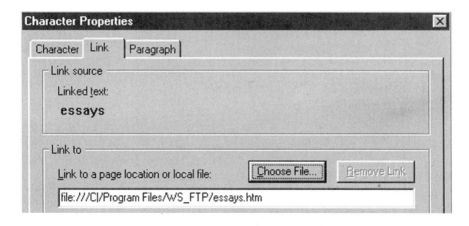

To create a hot link to your e-mail address, simply highlight the text or image you want as a link and insert the MAILTO command instead of a Web page address. The MAILTO command looks like this: mailto:login@server.address

---

PLACING YOUR PAGES ON THE SERVER

Once you have completed the design work and debugging for your first Web pages, the next step is to upload them to the server that will store them and make them available for viewing via the World Wide Web. Colleges, universities, and commercial Web sites have special instructions and policies regarding the proper uploading and maintenance of Web pages. In most cases you will use an FTP (File Transfer Protocol) client program to upload your HTML, GIF, or JPEG files to the server. An FTP client is a program that will allow you to move a copy of your Web page from your computer onto the server.

Most FTP programs have a window divided into two sections. The left-hand side is a listing of the directories or folders on your computer. The right-hand side is a listing of directories in your part of the server. Between the two window sides are two buttons, one pointing to the left and one pointing to the right. These buttons are used to direct file transfer from your system to the server and vice versa. To move a page to the server, take these steps:

1.   Use the local side of the window to locate the HTML file you created and saved on your hard drive or floppy drive.

2.   Use the server side of the window to locate the directory on the server where you wish to place your HTML files. Your help desk staff or instructor can provide you with instructions on how to access a directory designated for your HTML files.

3.   Select the files you want to transfer, and click on the button that moves them to the server.

For more information about uploading your Web pages, contact your local system administrator or help desk personnel.

 # HTML CODE CHECKERS

After you've spent hours and hours creating your Web site, you will want to be sure it does not contain missing links, incorrect tags, or other glitches. As you know by now, small errors such as leaving out a slash mark in an end tag or a closed quote symbol can affect a whole HTML page. If you are having trouble finding an error that plagues your page, or even if you think your code is perfect, you can use one of the computerized HTML validators to detect oversights and errors. The following are several of the checkers that offer free analysis.

http://imagiware.com/RxHTML.cgi

http://www.netmechanic.com

http://www.unipress.com/cgi-bin/WWWeblint

http://validator.W3.org

You can find additional sites by searching for HTML code checkers in a search engine.

 # THINGS TO REMEMBER

1. Constructing your first Web pages is a journey of exploration. You may have an idea of what effects you want, but you need to find the techniques that will allow you to create those effects. This chapter gives you an overview of only some of many techniques you can try.

2. Spend time exploring others' Web pages and looking at the source code for the pages. You can learn much from what others have invented.

3. You can easily "borrow" images from other sites on the Internet, but you need to secure permission to do so. Otherwise, you run the risk of copyright violation. The same is true of scanning photos from books; unless your obtain permission, you are violating copyright law. Many individuals and organizations who have Web pages are quite courteous about allowing students to borrow images. Simply send an e-mail to the site author's address listed on the home page and request permission. Many will reply immediately with permission and will ask only that you acknowledge the image source and perhaps include a link to the original page.

4. Explore graphics programs and learn their capabilities. If you know what kinds of effects are possible, you will generate more creative ideas for your pages.

5. Explore the Web itself for further instruction on how to construct Web pages. A more extensive list of sites than given earlier is included in Appendix 2.

6. Web pages are rarely finished. If you construct a nucleus of a few pages that are well-designed and executed in interesting ways, you can continue to add and change as long as the project holds your interest.

Working the Web

Appendix

Appendix

APPENDIX 1

Student Reviews of Web Sites

AARP
http://www.aarp.org

Are you a baby boomer looking for information about life after fifty? If so, there's a Web site just for you. It's the American Association of Retired Persons, better known as AARP. In case you're not familiar with AARP, it's a non-profit organization that describes itself as "dedicated to helping older Americans achieve lives of independence, dignity, and purpose."

The main page features a menu bar of four different categories. Each category contains information concerning a variety of topics. For example, when you click on the *Getting Answers* bar, there's up-to-date information about topics such as Health, Work and Economic Security, Independent Living, and Technology. From travel fraud to smart investing, it's a category that is sure to be of interest to everyone.

If you like what you see and want information about joining a local AARP chapter, just click on *Connections*, and you'll get the information you need. You can also find out about some of the community programs AARP offers such as Tax Aide and the 55 Alive/Mature Driving course, both designed to help boomers save money and maintain safe driving skills.

Beneath the main page menu bar, the site also includes a *Featured Topics* section which offers information of current interest. For example, if you want to find out the latest computer products, including software, you can discover what's available and how well it rates.

After logging onto the AARP for the first time, don't be surprised if you find yourself coming back to it repeatedly. It provides lots of valuable information that is designed to keep baby boomers well connected.

Kathy Barnhill, 1998

African Studies WWW Server

http://www.sas.upenn.edu/African_Studies/AS.html

This page hails from the University of Pennsylvania and is compiled by Professor Sandra T. Barnes, director of the African Studies Center. Included at the beginning of the home page are subheadings offering information about the University of Pennsylvania and its African Studies Department. Dr. Barnes has not filled the site with graphics; instead the focus is on providing an extensive list of topics and links covering virtually every aspect of African Studies. Included among them are a K–12 Africa Guide, Direct Feeds from Africa, Multimedia Archives, What's New in African Studies, and many others. The K–12 Guide offered information for both students and teachers, including information on the spoken languages of Africa, a linguistic analysis of some of the languages, and information regarding traveling to and within Africa.

The Black/African Internet Resources section provides links to subjects as diverse as Ethiopia, Hip Hop Rap, Dr. Martin Luther King, and issues on African Economy. It is clear that Dr. Barnes and her staff at the University of Pennsylvania have put in many hours of research to provide those interested in African studies a thorough and up-to-date look at what the Internet has to offer.

Randi Enloe, 1996

Amazon.com

http://www.amazon.com

Never again will you have to worry about finding a book or a musical recording. Amazon.com is *the* source for hard-to-find books or CDs. While there are many sites on the Web which offer books for sale, none can compete with Amazon.com when it comes to convenience, selection, and price.

Amazon.com is an extremely user-friendly site. It is divided into two major sections: Books and Music. It offers a "first-time visitors" section which helps those not familiar with online shopping. This section features links to instructions for finding a book or CD, ordering the merchandise, and delivery times. The main book page lets you shop your way. It offers a book search, browsing, a list of best-sellers, books which have been featured prominently in the media, a gift center (very handy for Christmas), a kids section, and even a recommendation center. Amazon offers over three million titles! They will even search for out-of-print books through their network of stores which sell used books. Amazon not only provides a synopsis of a book, but offers book reviews written by their customers. They will even offer you the chance to review a book and print that review on their site.

The music main page is very similar to the books main page. It has sections for music search, browsing, chart toppers, music featured prominently in the media, and a recommendation center. The search is divided into popular and classical music. You may browse music by style, artist, composer, or title. If it is hard to find, you'll probably find it here!

Amazon.com is not just comprehensive and convenient. It has what may be the best prices available for both books and music. You may expect to save from 20 to 40 percent on almost every selection available, sometimes even more! The shipping and handling fees are minimal and delivery time averages between 4 and 8 days.

Amazon.com is absolutely the best place to go when you need a hard-to-find book or CD. If you have a little patience and don't mind waiting a week, it can also be the best place to do your everyday shopping for books or CDs. If you can't find it, Amazon.com can.

J. Michael Mullins, 1998

BANK OF AMERICA

http://www.bankamerica.com

More and more businesses are finding the Web useful not only to display information about themselves, but as a way to offer consumer services while providing a link to their own services to gain these new customers. Bank of America is one of many banks conducting such business on the Web.

With an eye-catching initial logo and icons to find instant access to services, this page is inviting from the start. Choose from the Money Tip of the day, What's New, or one of the 11 icons that provide services like Special Offers, Personal Finance, Business Banking, Corporate Issues, Spare Change, Community, or Economics.

More detailed services include Credit Cards, Loans, HomeBanking, At-Home Checking, Savings and Investments, and a Student Union in which to offer special services to college students.

In the Corporate and Business Banking services, Capital Raising, Cash Management, Trade Services, Foreign Exchange, Risk Management, Investments, Merchant Services, Government Services, and the Private Bank offer detailed assistance in these and other specialized areas.

Under the heading of Community there is ample information regarding the corporation's Community Development in addition to the topic of the Environment if such aspects are criteria for consumer preferences. All told, the Bank of America Web page is well designed, well thought out, and presented professionally, well representing the banking institution.

Stephen M. Myers, 1996

BEVERLY HILLS

http://www.travelshop.com/trvshop3.htm

Calling all shopaholics! Come one, come all to the Beverly Hills travelshop home page. With its awesome, intense color graphics and a "no nonsense" direct column of links, it was easy to find this page irresistible.

The overall form of this site can be summed up in one world—adorable. Contained on the home page is a Beverly Hills "street directory," where you can choose to "visit" some of the prestigious locations in Beverly Hills. Santa Monica Boulevard, Beverly Drive, Brighton Way, and, of course, Rodeo Drive are just a few of the options. Enter the Beverly Drive link and explore some of the unique shops located there, or take a trip to Rodeo Drive, one of the most famous places on Earth.

When you select one of the destinations, you are presented with an extensive list of shops, boutiques, and eateries, complete with the address and phone number of each. In addition, you also have the option to "enter" inside some of the shops and see select pieces of merchandise.

If you visit Beverly Drive, you will encounter more of the everyday type of shop that includes Banana Republic and coffee shops galore. However, if it is glamour that you are seeking, then the Rodeo Drive link is the selection for you. Enter the Chanel boutique, and check out the upcoming colors and fashion designs that will be popular for the season. There's even a realistic photograph of the contemporary boutique that enables you to feel as if you are actually there. When you are finished visiting the shops, you then have the option of entering the link entitled "Attractions and Visitor Directory." This link contains numerous church, hospital, police, fire, post office, and chamber of commerce addresses and phone numbers.

This site was a lot of fun. It allowed me to explore such an expensive area for free. I was also able to explore a lot of areas in a short amount of time, and I didn't have to deal with traffic or crowds of people. So go "shopping" on Rodeo Drive, or anywhere else in Beverly Hills, and experience the glamour while learning more about the World Wide Web.

Carolyn Cannoy, 1996

BUK'S PAGE (CHARLES BUKOWSKI)

http://realbeer.com/buk/bio.html

On March 9, 1994, the world lost one of its great writers when the legendary lowlife Los Angeles poet Charles Bukowski (buk) died. Now, legions of his ever-growing fans can hang their coats at buk's page. It's divided into four sections: Letters, Ordering, Art, and Sure. First off, the user gets an extended biography of buk's life and a list of his more than 25 books in print.

The Letters section is full of people offering Bukowski anecdotes, jokes, or retelling how they eulogized him when news spread throughout the world of his death.

If you're having a hard time locating *Post Office* of a hardback edition of *The Rooming House Madrigals: Early Selected Poems 1946–1966,* fear not.

The Ordering section taps you directly into the bookstore A Clean Well Lighted Place, which serves up 24 books by Bukowski, including collections of poems, short stories, novels, and essays. You can order right on the screen.

Under Art, the user gets a small sampling of the writer's line drawings, which he often doodled on letters and manuscripts. Since 1991, Ed Smith has published annually *Sure: The Bukowski Newsletter.* In this section, the user gets to sample articles and images from back issues. Even for the most ardent Bukowski junkie, there's always something new.

Lawrence Welsh, 1996

THE CASE

http://www.thecase.com

If you are an Agatha Christie or Sherlock Holmes lover, this site is for you. The Case is a free interactive miniseries that provides the cyberspace detective with the Case, the Clues, and the Solution to a weekly mystery. You can become a detective as you read the history of the case, examine the clues, and (when you finally give up or think you have a solution) test your hypothesis against the true solution. The site also contains five previous cases for you to browse through if you solve the current case at detective speed.

Graphics, such as a magnifying glass in the heading and link boxes with fingerprints on them, just add to the feel of detective work and the whole "Sherlock Holmes" world. The weekly case was the Case of the Ghostly Killer when I visited the site, and the clues and solutions for the case were available. Visit the site. It is fun, challenging, entertaining, and a mystery to all who don't take time to visit.

Paula Woods, 1996

THE COMPLETE WORKS OF WILLIAM SHAKESPEARE

http://the-tech.mit.edu/Shakespeare

For those Shakespearean buffs surfing the Net, they need not surf anymore. This ode to the Bard himself offers not only full text of all his plays and many poems, but much, much more.

A plethora of links are provided, including Bartlett's familiar Shakespearean quotations, a Shakespeare discussion area, a glossary for all those words you never understood in high school, and two listings of his plays: one in chronological order, and the other in alphabetical order. The format of each play is similar and very user-friendly. Each individual play lists the acts and scenes with a brief one-sentence description. To actually read the scene, you only have to click on that scene. At the top of the page, there are links to go back to the home page or to go directly to the next scene. Many words that are not commonly understood have links to the glossary.

Although there is not much visual appeal (I only encountered one picture of Shakespeare), the volume of information is enormous, yet easy to read. Encountering this site makes you wish you were back in your high school senior English class reading one of Shakespeare's plays so that you could dazzle your teacher with brilliance.

Jill Goldmann, 1996

THE COPYRIGHT WEBSITE

http://www.benedict.com

This site has a wealth of information about issues related to the Internet. It discusses what is protected in Web publishing such as content, design, or link lists. It answers questions, such as what can you use from someone else's Web pages? What would constitute copyright violation? In the discussion of design, for example, the underlying design of a Web page consists of a certain arrangement of text, graphic, audio, video, VRML, etc.; and as long as that arrangement is original and non-trivial, the design of the page will be protected by copyright.

In link lists, a similar situation holds for the telephone book. As a list of names, addresses, and phone numbers, a phone list is not copyrightable under a compilation copyright because the fact that the listings were alphabetized was not original enough. But in link listings, if there is some original thought put into creating a link list, then it may be protectable. There is a host of information available on this subject, and it is tricky at best!

Judy Jimenez, 1996

COURT TV

http://courttv.com

Do you love a gripping courtroom drama? "Court TV's Web" site might be just the place for you. Graphics are plain but enough to be interesting. The format is well organized and neat: It must have been done by a lawyer.

The menu includes hot links to "Sites of the Week," "Menendez Updates," and "Weekly Contest." There are no graphics at "Sites of the Week," so if you like picture books, this might be too ho-hum for you. I like not having too much to look at, since it is hard enough sometimes trying to pick which link to follow. Clicking on any of the menu items takes you to other sites on the Web that are related to legal issues.

For instance, if you take the Hitchhiker's Guide to the Supreme Court, you are led to a sampling of cases that have been argued before the Supreme Court. Click on any one of these and you will find summaries of these arguments and the outcomes. Criminal law buffs will like the index entitled "A Guide to Prisoner-Related Resources." It leans heavily toward prisoner rights and includes an index of Listservs, Usenet newsgroups, online journals, magazines, and more.

What to become an American? Try the Immigration Assistant link. This site has a comprehensive list of online immigration law resources. Lawlinks takes you to a good general source of links to legal sites on the Web. These sites are changed weekly, so there's always something new to explore here.

Back at the home page, you can click on Weekly Contest for a chance at winning a Court TV T-shirt. Just answer the weekly trivia question via e-mail to be in the running.

Inside Court TV provides background information about this channel, including a program guide and a listing of educational services. The link to Court TV Kids is a page directed to the younger audience. It suggests links to other sites with topics about the law directly affecting kids.

You can Get Legal Help from this site or read Case Files of different ongoing trials on "Court TV." If you watch "Court TV" and have missed a verdict of a particular case, you can get that information here, too. Other links include Law Library, Court TV Games, and Court TV Store.

Diane Allen, 1996

THE ELECTRONIC FRONTIER FOUNDATION

http://www.eff.org

Space really was not the final frontier. The Electronic Frontier Foundation (EFF) is devoted solely to the preservation of civil liberties in the areas of privacy, free speech, and access specifically to information on the Internet. They are the sponsors of the "Blue Ribbon Campaign" for free speech online.

The Blue Ribbon is posted on each page on the site and several varieties of the graphic are available for downloading (which also downloads the link to this site). A blue ribbon was chosen for the same awareness technique that the red ribbon did for AIDS and the pink ribbon for breast cancer. The Blue Ribbon page has information about joining the coalition for free speech, most notably adding your name to the plaintiffs' list in the lawsuit that challenges the 1996 Telecommunications Act. Copies of the lawsuit, the Act, archives, and links to other sites are available. The home page has a table with clickable buttons in a table leading to About EFF, Alerts, Membership, Archives, Other Pubs & Info, and the Current Newsletter.

About EFF has a snail mail address, telephone number, and fax number along with the e-mail address. The page has information about EFF's purpose, how they monitor the online community to help preserve freedom of speech, and how they become actively involved in litigation to represent "netizens" (citizens on the Net) who are involved in freedom of speech or censorship entanglements.

The Membership page begins by telling you why you should join EFF and what kind of benefits you can expect. The form can be filled out interactively or can be downloaded in the HTML version or ASCII version.

The Archives page has a searchable index or you can use another clickable table listing several major indexes. Other Pubs & Info presents two more clickable tables with links to other publications and Internet sites, awards, sponsors, and a Usenet discussion group. The Current Newsletter immediately announces that it will take a few minutes to load. A bright purple graphic loads first with the name of the newsletter "EFFector." Ten volumes (including the current issue) can be accessed by yet another clickable table. March's issue has topics such as legislation on the Communications Decency Act, a "what you can do" section, Quote of the Day, and upcoming events.

The EFF Web site remains consistent throughout, utilizing the same color scheme (blue, white, and tan) and the clickable tables to list their links. Its main purpose is to relay information in text form about online communication, and it does this extremely well in short, concise, easy-to-read pages.

Barbara Kass, 1996

EPICURIOUS

http://www.epicurious.com

If you are interested in food, drink and travel then this is the right place for you Epicurious combines recipes from *Bon Appétit* and *Gourmet* magazines to tempt you and an extremely large beer, wine and spirits search index. Epicurious also offers a travel page that you can even book your flight from.

The recipe index offers more than 8,000 recipes and complete meal menus and adds hundreds more every month. Other than *Bon Appétit* and *Gourmet* the site also features *House & Garden* and new cookbooks that can be found in your nearest bookstore. Searching for recipes is made easy because you can type in keywords that range from Appetizers to Yogurt and everything in between. A section on how to prepare these recipes is also available if you are concerned about too much fat in your diet or only have enough time to throw something in the microwave.

The beer, wine and spirits index is quite extensive. You can take a quiz to test your knowledge on pouring, mixing and uncorking. Browsing through the Best Cellars search shows you wines from all over the world and the Greatest Hits search helps you to find the most popular wines. The site also helps you to find a good wine even if you don't have a lot of money to spend and they will even pick the drink for the meal you are planning to serve.

If traveling around the world is more interesting for you Epicurious and *Condé Nast Traveler* have what you need. All you have to do is enter your destination and the site will give you information on the airport, including its distance from your final destination, taxi service, money and exchange rates, possible hotels and their shuttle services and rental car availability. The airport code, time difference and cultural tips are also given. If you are interested, you can pick restaurants you want to visit wherever you may be traveling.

Epicurious offers a more specific search for travelers too. If you are looking at going to a beach or an island resort, a quaint bed and breakfast (in the U.S or

Canada) or a golf or ski resort, all the information you could ever need is right at your fingertips. If traveling to experience other cultures and their customs interests you then get into the World Events Calendar where you can find over 1,000 festivals around the world that are listed by region and month.

This site is quite large and holds an enormous amount of information, but it is very easy to find what you are looking for. Epicurious is divided into very specific areas that cater to whatever taste you have.

Meachell LaSalle, 1998

FACTSHEET FIVE

http://www.factsheet5.com

Known for years as the "bible of the zine scene," this site is a wired version of the legendary magazine *Factsheet Five*. But how'd it build its reputation? Each issue reviews dozens of small press zines and independent publications throughout the country. From the 19-year-old *Flipside* music/culture rag from Los Angeles to *Ben Is Dead*, a Low-Brow culture magazine, *Factsheet Five* covers turf completely ignored by the mainstream media.

This online addition is a virtual reproduction of the magazine, letting you canvas page after page of reviews. Visually, it lacks some of the pictures the magazine features, but all the copy is intact. In addition, the online version offers something the printed page doesn't: pointers for creating your own zine. Always at the forefront of the DIY (do it yourself) culture, FF bills itself as the guide to parallel culture. But what's that? According to the editor, it's stuff you might accidentally find, but can't locate through normal mainstream channels, like your local bookstore or supermarket.

Lawrence Welsh, 1996

GALERIE ART PARIS
AMERICAN ARTISTS IN PARIS

http://www.paris-anglo.com/gallery

Every month, Galerie Art Paris introduces the visual work of one or more American artists or photographers either working, living, or exhibiting in Paris. The exhibit begins with a graphic depiction of a room in a gallery that shows the work of the exhibitor being featured for that month. The viewer may click on a painting or sculpture shown at one of the three sides of the room to enter the exhibit. From there, the viewer may browse through the exhibit in the direction of his or her choice, as if in an actual gallery. The menu bar at the bottom of each piece of art gives options to receive information about the title, dimensions, and date of that particular work, or to get a closer look.

Overview is a survey of the exhibit. About the Artist offers biographical information on the artist, his or her education, exhibitions, and any videos or publications. In addition, there is information on how to contact the artist, to leave comments, or to purchase paintings. The Galerie Art Paris is an interactive site and an interesting venue for art buffs, art students who want to get a glimpse of what is selling in Paris, or collectors who are interested in purchasing paintings.

Randi Enloe, 1996

GRAND CANYON NATIONAL PARK

http://www.kaibab.org

The Grand Canyon National Park home page opens with a photo of a dramatic vista from this historical site. It gives information on its surroundings, history, services for tourists, activities at the canyon, its trails, many more helpful hints about visiting there, and general information about this national park. The graphics used show some spectacular sites at the Grand Canyon.

The Grand Canyon of the Colorado River is one of the seven natural wonders of the world. The rocks that make up the walls of the canyon range from 250 million years old at the top to over two billion years old at the bottom. Other historical information about different parts of the Canyon is also included. For instance, the Southern Rim mostly is a desert in which animals such as rock squirrels, ravens, mule deer, and other creatures are likely to be found. Often referred to as the "other" Grand Canyon is the Northern Rim. The scenery, climate, plants, animals, and even people are all different there. There is a much wetter climate to which the plant life has adapted. This section is much different from the southern part.

The site also offers directions on how to get to the Grand Canyon National Park. There is a wide variety of maps available of the Grand Canyon itself. One 3-D map shows the Colorado River, a variety of trails on particular sections of the canyon, and is in a full-size image. Other maps include an area map of Arizona, maps for each trail along with all other sections of the Grand Canyon. A guided tour is offered with pictures of sites that will be seen as a person embarks on the adventure. Other useful information like the weather is given for certain parts of the canyon, the Southern Rim, Northern Rim, and Inner Canyon.

This site is perfect for anyone interested in background and general information about the Grand Canyon. It is a big help for the tourist, as it gives directions and information needed for traveling through this natural wonder.

Christian Daw, 1996

HOT! HOT! HOT!

http://www.hothothot.com/hhh/index.shtml

It is only natural for chile lovers to search for the best hot sauce, one that will burn our tongues, cause our eyes to water, and bring upon us Montezuma's revenge. Hot! Hot! Hot!, the Internet's first "Culinary Headshop," is an online catalogue that allows you to order the sauces while surfing the Web.

Brought to you by Presence, Hot! Hot! Hot! has "over 100 products of fire," with names like Bats Brew, Nuclear Hell, and Ring of Fire. Sauces can be found by looking for them under heat level, origin, ingredients, or their name. Hot! Hot! Hot! also features a sauce of the month (this month's is "Jump Up and Kiss Me"). There are also several links to other related sites, such as *Chile Pepper Magazine* link.

For those hot food lovers, Hot! Hot! Hot! is where "you'll find fiery foodstuffs you never thought existed." The vibrant graphics that accompany the sauces are eye-catching in their simplicity. Rated as a top five percent Web site, Hot! Hot! Hot! lives up to this honor. Ordering your favorite hot sauce while online just made surfing the Net that much more fun.

Jill Goldmann, 1996

INTERESTING IDEAS

http://www.interestingideas.com

Looking for a treatise on Don Knotts or the moral economy of Mayberry? How about a collection of roadside art, including signs for White Castle gut burgers? Then jump on over to Bill Swislow's home page.

As a site designer for the *Chicago Tribune*, Swislow has created a visually stunning site, complete with a gallery of his own back-road photographs. Forget about boring family vacation shots. Swislow's more interested in Texas shotgun shacks and highway signs shouting out, "Good News! Fried Dough!"

He's also assembled more than a dozen shots of outsider folk art, from folks living in Alabama and Georgia. Outside of the gallery, the viewer can get a different take on the oftentimes vapid appraisal of pop culture. Swislow, for example, doesn't view the Cleavers from *Leave It to Beaver* as the perfect '50s American family: "A close inspection reveals a familial purgatory worthy of Tennessee Williams—toned down for TV, certainly, but still consumed with rage, sexual turmoil and plain old mendacity. This family needs help."

Visually arresting photographic reproduction, coupled with in-depth articles straight from Swislow's pen, makes this one of the most alluring and bizarre home pages I've visited.

Lawrence Welsh, 1996

THE INTERNET HERALD . . .

http://www.iherald.com

The Internet Herald, A Journal of News and Commentary by Generation X, is a home page devoted to issues of politics, music, poetry, and entertainment from the perspective of guess who, Generation X. The visual appeal of the Herald is pleasing because of the use of color and graphics.

The heading colors suggest a relationship to our world; blue, for clean air and water; green, for trees and grass; and yellow, which relates to the sun. The home-page is so large that you must scroll down to see all the page, but that is because of the attractive graphics used to call attention to the links. The graphics use a wide variety of colors and pictures, and it is clear the designers took their time when designing this fascinating site.

Bruce King, 1996

ISLAMIC TEXTS AND RESOURCES METAPAGE

http://www.buffalo.edu/student-life/sa/muslim/isl/isl.html

"In the Name of God, the Most Compassionate, the Most Merciful" begins Islamic Texts and Resources MetaPage. The green faux-marble background and Islamic logo create eye appeal and contribute an eastern flavor to this site. However, other than this one graphic, this is a text-only site, offered as a service by the University of Buffalo. Its purpose is to provide information about Islam and Islamic thought rather than about the culture and politics of Muslim peoples.

The organization of the site is clear and easy to follow, if somewhat plain. The reader who wants to know more about Muslim culture is offered the link The Muslim World—Culture, News and Issues forums. Clicking on this link takes you to another Web site, a black-and-grey, text-only resource page where you can select from a variety of topics to browse. These range from The Americas to History, Newsgroups, and Issues Concerning Muslims. Clicking on any of these topics does not produce a page about that subject; rather it takes you to an index of resources on the Net about the subject. The lists appear to be fairly comprehensive and include such topics as Muslims in Sports and The Muslim's Survival Guide to Christmas.

Back at the Islamic Texts home page, there is a list of texts about Islam. You can explore wide-ranging topics such as Marriage Laws in Islam, Islam: Farrakhism and Malcolm X, and List of Halal Foods. I clicked on Being Muslim to find a page entitled The Basics of Islam and Being Muslim. This page was a humble effort, according to the author, to explain basic concepts, beliefs, and thoughts about Islam. The text was set on a mosaic-like background, adding to the Islamic ambience.

This site is good for the serious student doing research about Islam. Graphics are scarce, but the text is rich in data.

Diane Allen, 1996

JAVA

http://java.sun.com

For those of you out there who are UNIX, HTML, C+, and C++ fanatics, this site is for you. It is time to meet your newest best friend, Java. Java is a simple, object-oriented, distributed, interpreted, robust, secure, architecture-neutral, portable, high-performance, multi-threaded, and dynamic language. Java was developed to avoid the problems of upgrades to existing programs. Java makes programming easier because it is multithreaded, thus making it a universal language. This is a very informative and exciting site having to do with the latest in computer design.

Here you can find the latest HotJava Browser (must be downloaded first), which enables the viewer to actually see the moving objects designed with the Java language. There is also an 80-page technical overview of the Java language and the browser. And for those of us who do not understand all of these languages, the site can also show you how to use Java and really understand it.

The site is very well organized with lots of help and FAQs. The links on the home page glide onto the page from every direction, giving you a sneak peek of what Java design is like. The What's New link contains the JAVAWORLD magazine (http://www.javaworld.com). This magazine is published online first and only online. Now, without further ado, go out and meet your new best friend, Java.

Erica Corral, 1996

Ludwig Van Beethoven

http://www.ida.his.se/ida/~a94johal/beethoven/beet.html

As a music lover, I naturally love to "surf" through the many Web pages that have something to do with music. I found this page very interesting as will anyone who likes classical music, knows about classical composers, or likes music history. By looking at this page you will learn that Beethoven was born in Germany in 1770, and his mother was a singer for the Elector of Köln. His father drank too much but was still able to see the talent in his son. He was disappointed, though, when he did not turn out to be a child prodigy like Mozart.

It is interesting to find out that Beethoven held a position as an assistant organist in the Electoral chapel; this is where he got his first lesson in composing. Sadly he did not live to finish all of his works. He was mourned by a large crowd at his funeral, and a single word is on his tombstone, Beethoven.

This page is set up very nicely; it starts by telling you a little about Beethoven, and provides a link to his mother and a link to his father. These links have biographical information on both of them, plus pictures. By going farther down the page, you will find a picture of Beethoven followed by more information. There are two more pictures, and then the page closes with a link to Beethoven's works. By clicking on this link, you will find a listing of all of the music composed by Beethoven, and some of these are linked to other pages. By clicking on these you will find a history of whatever work you choose.

This page is very informative, and I found it very interesting to find all of these facts on one of my favorite composers. It shocked me to find that in this modern age of computers, we can still learn about classical music, and by using the computer too.

Jinetta Fiscus, 1996

MEDSCAPE

http://www.medscape.com

Medscape is "the online resource for better patient care." Although the site is meant to be accessed primarily by physicians and students in the health professions, anybody who has the potential of ever being a patient might care to take a look in order to be better informed. Medscape features peer-reviewed articles, news, self-assessment, and a search engine. The graphics are small and concise. For example, the AIDS section has a clickable icon of the red ribbon. In addition, Medscape makes excellent use of bold and enlarged typeface as well as lines to divide sections.

Upon accessing Medscape, you will be prompted to create an account. Medscape is free to everyone, but requires you to register with an ID (user name) and password. If you ever forget your password, you can simply create a new account.

The home page opens with Today's Question (for example, is chronic pyelonephritis the result of chronic or acute bacterial infection?) and a clickable Answer. (The answer is no, it is the result of repeated episodes of infection that lead to scarring—aren't you relieved to know this?" The Answer page gives the source and author of the answer.

Also on the home page are the sections entitled Topics, News, Journals, and Test Yourself. Each of these is in the form of a graphic that looks like a file folder with the headings on the tabs.

Topics include AIDS, infectious disease, managed care, oncology, surgery, urology, and women's health. The News section features the most recent articles from the *Medical Tribune News*, health briefs, AIDS, columns on topics such as nutrition, and editorials (also known as the shoot-your-mouth-off section). The Journals area includes the AIDS Reader, Drug Benefit Trends, Infections in Medicine, and Medical Tribune, The Test Yourself page has PicTours (actual photos for show-and-tell), Bug of the Month (which gives a list of symptoms and then prompts the physician for the answer), the Today's Question, archives of questions, and Continuing Education programs.

The search option allows the user to limit the time of the article (i.e., the oldest article available on the topic to the most recent). The search returns articles from magazines, journals, and the Morbidity and Mortality Weekly Report.

For a site that has an enormous amount of medical information, Medscape is easy to access with clear instructions and information that is divided into understandable subtopics. Its sources are reliable and anyone can count on the information presented as accurate and timely.

Barbara Kass, 1996

MOVIE POSTERS ARCHIVE

http://anubis.science.unitn.it/services/movies/index.html

Webmaster Valter Cavecchia, who runs sites dedicated to a series of science fiction films (*Alien* and *Blade Runner*) digs deep into another aspect of Hollywood—its marketing posters. What gives this site its legendary ranking is its attention to old Hollywood. I mean, who wants to see a poster for *Ghost Busters* when the 1959 classic *Anatomy of a Murder* is available? If you're wondering what the poster for the 1938 *Angels with Dirty Faces* looked like, let Valter take you on this wired trip. And since our Web host is into the Sci-Fi game, there are plenty of *Star Trek* tributes and posters of other space travel movies from Hollywood's yesteryears.

Fortunately, the reproduction is high quality. Of course you can't get the size and depth of the real thing, but this is still paradise for someone who wants to get lost in the vaults of Hollywood.

Lawrence Welsh, 1996

THE OFFICIAL X-FILES WEB SITE

http://www.thex-files.com

The Fox Network television show, *The X-Files*, has developed quite a cult following of dedicated fans over the last few years. As a result, "*X-Files* internet shrines," or web sites, abound. One such site, a "must-bookmark" site, is the Official X-Files Web Site, sponsored and maintained by Twentieth Century Fox Film Corporation.

This site has everything to excite and delight even the most dedicated *X-Files* groupies, known affectionately as "X-Philes." The heart of the site contains the most important information on the television show: an Episode Guide, which gives a synopsis of every episode of *The X-Files* ever aired, listed by season and air date; a background overview of the show, with hints for what is to come in the next season; and bios on the characters, actors, staff, producers, and the show's creator, Chris Carter. The "bio" section also features awards the show has won and a brief fact sheet on the show.

The fans are important to the success of the show, and this aspect has carried over to the web site. There is a message board for fans to discuss episodes, ask questions, and exchange information with other X-Philes. There is also a section that provides details and pricing for anyone who wishes to join the fan club. The most exciting features is that fans are able to order merchandise and collectibles directly from the producers. The *X-Files* game, album, episode videos, books, alien statues, the official *X-Files* magazine, and anything else ever manufactured can all be found here, along with ordering information and prices.

Other features of this site include quick-time trailers from *The X-Files Movie*, a search engine for locating information within the site, and a mail area where fans can send *X-Files* postcards, via email, to other X-Philes. There is also a "What's New" section, which lists new areas of the site, updates on the show, new merchandise or collectibles, and any other new information of interest to fans.

This site is set up so that even the amateur net surfer will have no problem finding what they are looking for. Each section is clearly labeled and linked from the main page, and it is very easy to navigate from one area to the next. Silver-gray text on a black background, coupled with great pictures from the show, make up a site that is dramatic, but uncluttered and easy on the eyes.

The Official X-Files Web Site is one of the best *X-Files* Internet shrines available on the World Wide Web. Because it is attractive, easy to navigate, and contains everything anyone ever wanted to know about *The X-Files*, any X-Phile, or "X-Phile-in-training," will definitely want to spend hours exploring this great site.

Sandra Leanne Lopez, 1998

Rainforest Action Network

http://www.ran.org/ran

Founded ten years ago, the Rainforest Action Network (RAN) is a nonviolent, volunteer-based, nonprofit organization. They concentrate on saving the rainforests all over the world and the communities that surround them. They support the human rights of the people who make their homes in the forests. Their site has been listed as one of Yahoo!'s cool sites, and when you see their page, you can understand why. They use great graphics and pictures, and the site is very user-friendly and informative.

When you open RAN's page, you are greeted with a colorful screen with the RAN logo. There is a list of links to follow, each done very creatively. For example, the Tribal link has a colorful totem pole design.

The Campaigns link, for example, informs you about programs the organization is currently working on. At present, they are boycotting Mitsubishi and Texaco. The pages explain why they are boycotting each company and information about what individuals can do.

The Kid's Corner tells kids, in terms that they will understand, what they can do to save the rainforests. They can learn about life in the rainforest by reading about the forest itself, the people who live there, or the animals. There is a glossary for terms that kids might not understand, and a question-and-answer section.

I found this site to be very informative without being too overbearing. The information is presented to you, and you have the choice to either do something or go on. The graphics are outstanding!

Rachael Mendoza, 1996

The Rocky Horror Picture Show

http://www.insv.com/rhps

Audience participation and an outrageously good time is what the *Rocky Horror Picture Show* is all about. This movie is filled with nothing but humor, and people around the globe flock to midnight showings in order to show their *Rocky Horror Picture Show* pride.

Audience participation started in the '80s, and you can read all about its history under the participation link. You can also obtain knowledge of the prop usage and Rocky etiquette. People take props such as newspapers and toilet paper in order to add more to the film. Several lines are also shouted out by the audience during the movie that are basically the same across the country. A list of these lines can also be found under the participation link.

The *Rocky Horror Picture Show* had its twentieth anniversary recently, and one of the links is devoted to the development of the film over the years. Letters from past impersonators and a theater list are interesting reading material in this link. If you are a die-hard Rocky fan you can purchase Rocky memorabilia through this Web site.

This site fits the movie because of the cartoon drawings and the Rocky lips everywhere. There are not many graphics, but the logo lips appear on practically every link. I found this site interesting and informative because I love the *Rocky Horror Picture Show*. If you are a virgin, which means you have never been to see the movie, then this site may seem kind of strange and may not make much sense, but once you see the movie, you will probably be hooked for life.

Rene Irene Ortega, 1996

Sex, Censorship and the Internet

http://www.eff.org/CAF/cafuiuc.html

This is an excellent site for those overseeing Internet access in the workplace or academic settings. Webmaster Carl M. Kadie reminds the reader on issues of First Amendment rights, what would actually be considered "obscene" material, academic policies, and actual case citations. With page links entitled Introduction, Current Policies & Experience, Academic Freedom, Two Types of Acceptable Use Policies, Applying Academic Freedom to Academic Computers, Top Intellectual Freedom Policies, The Case of NYX, The Case of CICA, The Case of the Greek List, The Case of the Free-Net, The Case of Iowa State Univ., The Case of V-Chip, The Case of CERT, The Case of K–12. At the beginning, a hypothetical question of whether students should be punished for using vulgarities on the Net is posed. The answers are not simple, but the Webmaster explores experiences of public libraries, student newspapers, and computer facilities at other universities. Under introduction, the question of what is "obscene" is tackled. Links to several universities and various newsgroups are explored.

Elizabeth Fouran, 1996

The Shania Twain Page

http://www.shania.com

When thinking of the newest country music artists, one cannot help but think about the fastest rising, new female artist Shania Twain. With her latest releases including the upbeat, fun songs: "Any Man of Man," "Whose Bed Have Your Boots Been Under," "If You're Not in It For Love," and, the latest, "You Win My Love," she has taken the music world by storm. She also has a beautiful love song called "The Woman in Me."

This page contains several links to other pages. You can choose to look at Shania's picture page, biography, lyrics, or even get samples of two of her songs. There is even a link where you can sign up for her mailing list.

After linking to the biography page, you will find that Shania is Ojibway for "I'm on my way," which is such an appropriate name for this young, beautiful, talented lady. She has surprised the country music industry with her almost overnight success. This page is a fun page to check out. There are also many more pages like this, including pages for George Strait, Garth Brooks, Trisha Yearwood, and many others. These pages are definitely worth checking out if you like country music.

Jinetta Fiscus, 1996

STONES WORLD

http://www.stonesworld.com

Looking for Satisfaction? If you're a Rolling Stones fan (or fanatic) this is the spot. While they're not as young as they once were, the self-proclaimed bad boys of rock 'n' roll are up-to-the-minute hipsters when they move to the wired front.

After performing last year in an online concert, the Stones recently unveiled an "official" Web site that puts other musical acts to shame. But here's the kicker: Unless your own the top techno toys, you might not be able to tap all the available options, like the streamable songs, which require ISDN or faster. But if you need to know what album first featured "Sweet Black Angel" or what Stone recorded the solo album "Monkey Grip," you're in the right location.

You can even try your luck at cards. Go ahead, see if you can whip Keith Richards at five-card stud. No matter which Stone you go up against, the challenge is formidable.

Lawrence Welsh, 1996

UNIVERSITY OF REGENSBURG

http://www.uni-regensburg.de

A page away from home—as a student from a foreign country, I have a hard time staying in contact with my hometown. The precious time I spend on the phone is used for personal and family-related subjects. I consider myself lucky since I have access to the World Wide Web and the university located in my hometown has a WWW page.

The home page greets me in my native language and makes me feel right at home. The first and most important stop is Aktuelles, the news of the university. This has short information items, organized by dates of upcoming important events. An online version of *RIZ*, the Regensburg University Newspaper, is also found here. With articles about the latest news and ongoing problems, this medium gives you a firsthand look at the continuing controversies on the Regensburg campus.

The first part is followed by a listing of available institutions, ranging from the library to the clinic, followed by information about departments and the degree plans they offer. If you're interested in obtaining a degree at the University of Regensburg, this is the place to look.

Important to me is the link to the Gerd Boehms gopher, created by a student, which gives news about the social life of Regensburg, including a social calendar and a sporting events table, as well as links to other Regensburg gophers. This is the place for me to stay in touch with home, bringing news I am not able to get anywhere else.

Martin G. Schmidt, 1996

VIRTUAL SEMINARS FOR TEACHING LITERATURE

http://info.ox.jtap/

Educated English gentlemen enlisted quickly, chivalrously eager to serve their noble country. They died just as quickly in a war that never seemed to move, or to end, or to make any sense. During the course of World War I, an entire language changed thanks to the soldier poets who found that the language of King Arthur which had sent them to war could not help them describe the experience of war.

The BBC News Online: Education section describes this Web site as a project devised by the head of Oxford University's Centre for Humanities Computing, Dr. Stuart Lee. Funded by JISC Technology Applications, this site is free to the general public as a condition of the funding. People studying World War I literature can follow virtual seminars with manuscripts, photos, and audio and visual clips. The main intention of the site is to offer complete access to original material that is scattered around the world, and which would be almost impossible to accumulate any other way.

The first seminar introduced in 1995 was "Isaac Rosenberg's 'Break of Day in the Trenches.'" Students were invited to record their reactions to Rosenberg's poem, and then browse hypermedia pages of analysis and contextual information about the poet, trench warfare, casualties and other contemporary writers.

Today, the site includes the complete original manuscripts of *The Hydra*, a journal produced at the Craiglockhart Military Hospital where Wilfred Owen was treated, all the manuscripts of Owen's war poetry and some of his letters and photographs—all using HTML frames. There are also approximately 100 audio clips, 50 video clips from film shot in 1916 and about 500 photographs, as well as an extremely rare audio clip of Siegfried Sassoon reading one of his poems. Most notable is the fact that this site makes copyrighted works freely available through negotiations with various institutions.

The main resources available are "The Seminars," "The Wilfred Owen Multimedia Digital Archive" and *The Hydra*. There are also links to "Poppy Appeal," the

"Royal British Legion," the "Remembrance Page," "More World War I and Poetry Links" and "Search the Site."

Judith A. Fourzan, 1998

THE WHITE HOUSE

http://www.whitehouse.gov

Regardless of who or which party occupies the White House, everyone should know the address on the Internet as well as the historical 1600 Pennsylvania Avenue. Once you have connected to the Web site, there are a host of options via simple icons that can both give and receive information that is important to the citizenry.

The Welcome page begins with a real logo treating the visitor like a special invited guest. The first icon offers the president and vice president, with information about their accomplishments, families, and how to send them electronic mail. The What's New calendar offered information concerning the president's State of the Union address in addition to a 45-page document on the itemized reasons he was declining the opposing party's budget. The Interactive Citizens' Handbook offers a guide to information and services from the federal government while additional icons provide White House history of past presidents and first families, art in the house, and tours from room to room. In the Virtual Library you can search White House documents, listen to speeches, and view photos, while in the Briefing Room you can discuss up-to-date releases, hot topics, and the latest government statistics. Have a question? Frequently asked questions and answers about the service are conveniently located within a question mark icon, plus the service is friendly for children, with an icon for kids to become more active and informed.

Perhaps the most fun of this page is the opportunity to sign the White House electronic guest book. There is also space for a 2500-word comment sheet should you wish to feed back any information about your experience online. Finally, a simple icon click on one of the four photos featuring the president, first lady, vice president and spouse will allow your instant e-mail to their specific attention. As in the old saying "The pen is mightier than the sword," you have much power by your participation in government by what access you have online with the White House Web page.

Stephen M. Myers, 1996

WHITE HOUSE TOURS

http://www.whitehouse.gov/WH/tours/visitors_center.html

This technologically sophisticated site has really expanded since the past few years and is up-dated regularly. Not only is there access to President Clinton's budget accomplishments and direct access to Federal Services, but the most recent addition to the site is a new link that tells how to become a White House Fellow and gives information on the White House Millennium Council. Furthermore, you can visit several other places: the Virtual Library which includes extensive archives of the White House documents, the Briefing Room which contains the latest news releases, hot topics and the latest federal statistics, and a section for kids that helps young people become more informed citizens.

The White House History and Tours link is of particular interest because this is where you can see rooms and furnishings from both past and present, also portraits of the Presidents and First Ladies of the US and the art in the President's house. From Tuesday through Saturday the White House is open for tours. These free tours can be visited in two ways: public self-guided tours and congressional tours. The self-guided tours are the most frequently used. Visitors can move from room to room at their leisure. From the ground floor, the Vermeil Room and the library can be seen, and upstairs is the state floor. For the Congressional Guided Tour you would need to reserve tickets in advance. It is appropriate for high school students and older. You do not have to be there to see the art work. It can be viewed on the website. Art in the White House features: Preface to Collections, Art for the President's House, Selected Works from the Collections and Art from Modern European Masters. You can choose to view paintings of subjects, people or landscapes. At this website you can see an oil painting by Paul Cezanne of "Still Life Quince and Pears" (1885). You can see the "Young Mother and Two Children" (1908) by Mary Cassatt and "The Mouth of the Delaware" (1828) by Thomas Birch. This painting was a gift from the White House Historical Association. All you have to do is click on more art and the exhibition continues until you have exhausted it all.

The purpose of this site was to inform and educate people. I found that the graphics were very well done. In fact, you have a choice to view the site in text form or graphics. It is like touring a museum from the internet. I enjoyed the art. The color of the paintings jump out at you. I highly recommend viewing this site.

Alfred La Piana, 1998

WORD

http://www.word.com/index.html

Word is a new-age computerized magazine published online. The page design is somewhat outrageous but somehow sophisticated and stylish. This site serves up some of the best kinetic Web art. It is capable of spinning its links around and flashing the viewer into new dimensions through the help of Java.

You may come across a set of flying lips and phrases that will make you think or laugh the whole day. With all the fun that comes with these pages, so do some articles, fiction, poetry, exhibits, photography, and astounding art. You can find these in a range of categories: habit, talk, desire, work, place, gigo (trash-out).

In the Desire section you can inter-relay chat with other magazine subscribers from a selection of interesting and somewhat crazy topics. Or you can create your own short page.

Erica Corral, 1996

THE WORD DETECTIVE

http://www.users.interport.net/~words1

"Words, Wit, Wisdom," a syndicated newspaper column that has been answering readers' questions about words and language since 1983 in the United States, Mexico, and Japan, is now accessible to Internet browsers. The column, originally started by William Morris, editor-in-chief of the first edition of the *American Heritage Dictionary*, is now accessible to millions of readers via the World Wide Web.

The column runs three times a week, and text of both the specific question about a word and the researched answer can be enjoyed by all when clicking on Content. The dialogue framework of this link makes learning both entertaining and interesting. A click on Previous Columns reveals text of the bi-monthly newsletter, The Word Detective. Words, Wit, Wisdom also contains some fun graphics and links to other English topics.

Paula Woods, 1996

APPENDIX 2

Sources of Additional Information

GENERAL WEB INFORMATION AND GUIDES

Discover System

http://classes.aces.uiuc.edu/ACES100.

EFF's (Extended) Guide to the Internet

http://www.eff.org/papers.eegtti

Exploring the World-Wide Web

http://www.gactr.uga.edu/exploring/index.html

A Guide to Cyberspace

http://www.hcc.hawaii.edu/guide/www.guide.html

Virtual Computer Library

http://www.utexas.edu/computer/vcl

World Wide Web FAQ

http://www.boutell.com/faq

The World Wide Web for the Clueless

http://www.mit.edu:8001/people/rei/wwwintro.html

WEB SEARCH GUIDES

General Finding Tools

http://lib-www.ucr.edu/pubs/navigato.html

Internet Search Tool Details

http://sunsite.berkeley.edu/Help/searchdetails.html

Understanding WWW Search Tools

http://www.indiana.edu/~librcsd/search

WebPlaces Internet Search Guide

http://www.webplaces.com

WEB PAGE AUTHORING GUIDES

Advanced Techniques

http://science.nas.nasa.gov/NAS/WebWeavers/advanced.html

Beginner's Guide to HTML

http://www.ncsa.uiuc.edu/General/Internet/WWW/HTMLPrimer.html

Crash Course in Writing Documents for the Web

http://www.pcweek.com/eamonn/crash_course.html

Frames Basics

http://home.netscape.com/navigator/v2.0/index.html

How to Write HTML

http://www.uwaterloo.ca/web-docs/Guidelines/howto.html

Learning HTML

http://www.bev.net/computer/htmlhelp/index.html

Library of Congress Internet Resource Page

http://lcweb.loc.gov/global/internet/html.html

Putting Information onto the Web

http://www.w3.org/pub/WWW/Provider/Overview.html

Style Guide for Online Hyptertext

http://www.w3.org/pub/WWW/Provider/Style/Overview.html

A Virtual Tool Box

http://www.netsurge.com/trillian/webbie.htm

The Web Designer

http://web.canlink.com/helpdesk

Webmaster Reference Library

http://www.webreference.com

STYLE GUIDES

Advice for HTML Authors

http://www.hwg.org/resources/html/style.html

Guide to Web Style

http://www.sun.com/styleguide/tables/Welcome.html

Web Style Manual (Yale)

http://info.med.yale.edu/caim/manual/contents.html

WORKING THE WEB

GLOSSARY

address The unique code assigned to a file stored at some location on a network.

ASCII (pronounced AS-key) American Standard Code for Information Exchange. Frequently used to denote plain text that can easily be converted into any word processing program.

backbone Network of high capacity connections between local networks.

bit The smallest amount of information that can be transmitted. A combination of bits can indicate an alphabetic character, a numeric digit, or another type of information.

boolean A query strategy for searching key-word databases. Uses connectors such as "and" or "or" to expand or narrow a search.

browser Application software that gives you a graphical interactive interface for searching, finding, and viewing information over a network.

CGI The Common Gateway Interface is an interface for programmers who build scripts or applications that run behind-the-scenes on a Web server. These scripts can generate text or other types of data, perhaps in response to input from the user or from retrieving information from a database.

client-Server A client program runs on your home computer. When you give instructions to the client program, it requests information from a remote computer running a server program.

compression/decompression A method of encoding/decoding information that allows transmission (or storage) of information in a more compact form.

connection A point-to-point dedicated or switched communication path between computers.

cyberspace Originally used in *Neuromancer*, a novel by science fiction author William Gibson, refers to the collective forms of computer-aided communication.

database A multi-user collection of information. Provides for organized storage and retrieval of large amounts of information.

dedicated line A private line leased from an Internet Service Provider carrier.

digital A device or method that uses discrete electrical variations to encode, process, or carry binary (zero or one) signals for sound, video, computer data, or other information.

download To transfer programs or data from a computer to a connected device, usually from a server to a personal computer

e-mail Electronic mail. Messages sent over computer networks.

FAQ Frequently Asked Question

flame An insult delivered by e-mail or a newsgroup posting.

frames Frame tags are used to break a Web page into two or more scrollable spaces. Each of these spaces has its own URL.

FTP (file transfer protocol) A protocol used to provide file transfers across a wide variety of systems.

GIF (graphics interchange format) GIF is a standard format for image files on the WWW. The GIF file format is popular because it uses a compression method to make files smaller.

Home The startup page of a site, containing identification and index information.

HTML (hypertext markup language) A "tag" language in which Web pages are formatted and Web information is distributed.

HTTP (hypertext transfer protocol) The method by which documents are transferred from the host computer or server to browsers on remote computers.

hyperlink Connections between one piece of information and another on the World Wide Web. Can be within documents or from one document to another.

hypermedia A method of presenting information in units connected by links. The information may be presented using a variety of media such as text, graphics, audio, video, and animation.

hypertext Describes a type of interactive online navigation functionality. Links (URLs) embedded in words or phrases allows the user to select a link and immediately display related information and multimedia material which may be in another document.

image map The use of an image with embedded links as a navigation device on a Web page.

IP (internet protocol) The Internet protocol that defines the unit of information passed between systems that provides for Internet communication.

IP address The Internet protocol address assigned to a computer.

ISDN (integrated services digital network) A set of standards for high-speed transmission of simultaneous voice, data, and video information.

Java An object oriented programming language similar to C++ which allows Web authors to add extra pizzazz to their pages.

JPEG (joint photographic experts group) JPEG is a popular method used to compress photographic images. Many Web browsers accept JPEG images as a standard file format for viewing.

link See Hyperlink.

listserv A subject-specific list maintained by an automated e-mail program. Participants subscribe to a list and via e-mail they exchange postings about the topic with other subscribers.

login An identification used to access a computer system.

modem (MODulator-DEModulator) End user computer interface that enables digital data to be transmitted over analog transmission line such as phone lines.

multimedia Computer systems that integrate audio, video and data.

network A system of interrelated elements that are interconnected to provide local or remote communication (of voice, video, data, etc.) and to facilitate the exchange of information between users with common interests.

newsgroups A large grouping of online discussion groups also called Usenet newsgroups.

page A hypermedia document on the Web

PPP (point to point protocol) Dial-up Internet connection speaking in TCP/IP protocol, somewhat faster than SLIP.

real time Rapid transmission and processing of information and transactions as they occur, in contrast to being stored and retransmitted.

server In a network, a host data station that provides facilities to other stations.

site Address location of a server on the Internet

SLIP (serial line internet protocol) Dial-up Internet connection speaking in TCP/IP protocol.

SSL The Secure Socket Layer is a protocol that Netscape uses to provide people with secure transactions over the network.

tables   Table tags are used to create blocks of text or images on a Web page within which information can be organized.

tags   HTML uses tags to shape and organize Web documents. Tags are set apart from the document by the use of angle brackets ($\langle\ \rangle$).

TCP/IP   Transmission Control Protocol/ Internet Protocol is the standard network communications protocol used to connect computer systems across the Internet.

Telnet   Telnet is a network program that offers a way to log into and work from another computer. By logging into another system, users can access Internet services that they might not have on their own computers.

URL (uniform resource locator)   The method of addressing data based on the name of the server where the site's files are stored, the file's directory path, and its file name.

Usenet   A bulletin board system of discussion groups called newsgroups. Usenet predates the World Wide Web, and postings can be read by a variety of software programs, including Web browsers.

VRML (virtual reality modeling language)   A "tag" language in which Web pages are formatted that can support 3D graphics and interactive spatial navigation.

WWW (world wide web)   Internet system for world-wide hypertext linking of multimedia documents, making the relationship of information that is common between documents easily accessible and completely independent of physical location.

CREDITS

Unless otherwise noted, the Website Domain Names (URLs) provided are not published by Harcourt College Publishers and the Publisher can accept no responsibility or liability for the content of these sites. Because of the dynamic nature of the Internet, Harcourt College Publishers cannot in any case guarantee the continued availability of third-party web sites. 11, 15, 16, 97, 98, 105, 106, 119 Netscape Communications Corporation has not authorized, sponsored, or endorsed, or approved this publication and is not responsible for its content. Netscape and the Netscape Communications Corporate Logos are trademarks and trade names of Netscape Communication Corporation. All other product names and/or logos are trademarks of their respective owners; 12, 17, 18, 98, 99, 108, 109 Boxshots reprinted with permission from Microsoft Corporation; 25 Copyright © 1999 BankAmerica Corporation; 27 Copyright © 1998 Deja.com, Inc. All rights reserved; 28 Reprinted by permission of the Electronic Frontier Foundation; 29 Copyright © 1999 Monster.com. All rights reserved; 30 Courtesy of Martin Luther King Jr. Papers Project; 32 Courtesy of Nasdaq Stock Market, Inc; 33 Copyright © 1999 The New York Times Company. Reprinted by permission; 34 Copyright © 1971–1999 Project Gutenberg, all rights reserved; 35 Copyright © 1995, 1996, 1997, 1998, 1999 Smithsonian Institution; 36 Copyright © 1999 SportsLine USA, Inc. All rights reserved; 37 Courtesy of Uproar; 44, 52 Text and artwork copyright © 1999 by Yahoo! Inc. All rights reserved. YAHOO! and the YAHOO! logo are trademarks of YAHOO! Inc; 45, 46, 47 Courtesy of Compaq Computers and AltaVista; 48 Courtesy of the American Health Network; 49, 51 Excite and Webcrawler are trademarks of Excite, Inc., and may be registered in various jurisdictions. Excite screen display copyright © 1995–1999 Excite, Inc; 49 Reprinted by permission. Infoseek, Ultrasmart, Ultraseek Server, Infoseek Desktop, Infoseek Ultra, Quickseek, Imageseek, Ultrashop, the Infoseek logos and the tagline, "Once you know, you know," are trademarks of Infoseek Corporation which may be registered in certain jurisdictions. Other trademarks shown are trademarks of their respective owners. Copyright © 1994–1999 Infoseek Corporation. All rights reserved; 50 Copyright © 1999 Lycos, Inc. All rights reserved. Lycos® is a registered trademark of Carnegie Mellon University; 52 Courtesy of The Hekman Library; 53, 55 Copyright © 1999 the Regents of the University of California. All rights reserved; 54 Copyright © 1995–1999 the Regents of the University of Michigan, Ann Arbor, MI; 54 Courtesy of the University of Wisconsin, Madison, Computer Sciences & Statistic Department; 57 Courtesy of Gerard Manning, Menlo Park, CA; 58 Copyright © 1999 Time, Inc. Reprinted by permission. Photo: copyright © 1999 Vince Parker/U.S. Air Force/AP/Wide World Photos; 100, 101 Courtesy of the Academic Computing Center, Office of Computing & Communication, University of Washington, Seattle; 104 ListServ® screen. Courtesy of L-Soft International; 155 Courtesy of the Ministry of Culture, Paris, France; 163, 164, 165 Image Composer 1.0 shots reprinted with permission from Microsoft Corporation.

INDEX